Red Books *showing the way*

LOCAL STREET ATLAS

PORTSMOUTH

G000293499

EMSWORTH · HAYLING ISLAND · HAVANT
HORNDEAN · PETERSFIELD · PORTCHESTER

CONTENTS

Page Layout & Road Map......................3
3 Miles to 1 Inch

Portsmouth Enlarged Centre............ 4-5
7 Inches to 1 Mile

Street Maps....................................... 6-37
4 Inches to 1 Mile

Index to Streets............................ 38-48

	Minor Road
	Pedestrianized / Restricted Access
	Track
	Built Up Area
	Footpath
	Stream
	River
Lock	Canal
	Railway / Station
●	Post Office
P P+	Car Park / Park & Ride
C	Public Convenience
+	Place of Worship
→	One-way Street
i	Tourist Information Centre
8 8	Adjoining Pages
	Area Depicting Enlarged Centre
	Emergency Services
	Industrial Buildings
	Leisure Buildings
	Education Buildings
	Hotels etc.
	Retail Buildings
	General Buildings
	Woodland
	Orchard
	Recreational / Parkland
	Cemetery

Every effort has been made to verify the accuracy of information in this book but the publishers cannot accept responsibility for expense or loss caused by an error or omission.

Information that will be of assistance to the user of the maps will be welcomed.

The representation on these maps of a road, track or path is no evidence of the existence of a right of way.

Street plans prepared and published by
Red Books (Estate Publications) Ltd, Bridewell House, Tenterden, Kent, TN30 6EP.
The Publishers acknowledge the co-operation of the local authorities of towns represented in this atlas.

Ordnance Survey® This product includes mapping data licensed from Ordnance Survey® with the permission of the Controller of Her Majesty's Stationery Office.

© Crown Copyright
© Red Books (Estate Publications) Ltd
ISBN 978-1-84192-426-7
069-17/02-06
All rights reserved
Licence Number 100019031

www.redbooks-maps.co.uk

WO2007

LOCAL STREET ATLASES contain comprehensive local coverage.
COUNTY STREET ATLASES contain street maps for each town centre.

CHICHESTER & BOGNOR REGIS

including: Aldwick, Barnham, Birdham, Bosham, East Wittering, Fishbourne, Fontwell, Hunston, Mid Lavant, Middleton-on-Sea, North Bersted, Pagham, Runcton, Selsey, Sidlesham, Tangmere, West Wittering, Westergate, Yapton etc.

FAREHAM & GOSPORT

including: Abshot, Bridgemary, Crockerhill, Elson, Hill Park, Lee-on-the-Solent, Locks Heath, Peel Common, Portchester, Privett, Sarisbury, Southwick, Stubbington, Titchfield, Warsash, West End, Wymering etc.

HAMPSHIRE

including: Aldershot, Alton, Andover, Ashurst, Basingstoke Centre, Bishop's Waltham, Bordon, Brockenhurst, Cosham, Cowplain, Denmead, Eastleigh, Emsworth, Fareham Centre, Farnborough, Fleet, Fordingbridge, Gosport, Hartley Wintney, Havant, Headley, Headley Down, Heath End, Hook, Hordle, Hythe, Kingsclere, Lee-on-the-Solent, Liphook, Liss, Lymington, Lyndhurst, Milford on Sea, New Alresford, New Milton, North Baddesley, Oakley, Petersfield, Portsmouth, Ringwood, Romsey, South Hayling, Southampton Centre, Totton, Waterlooville, Whitchurch, Wickham, Winchester Centre, Yateley etc.

SOUTHAMPTON

including: Ashurst, Bassett, Bishop's Waltham, Bishopstoke, Bitterne, Blackfield, Botley, Burridge, Bursledon, Buttsash, Cadnam, Calmore, Chandlers Ford, Colden Common, Dibden Purlieu, Eastleigh, Fair Oak, Fawley,, Hamble-le-Rice, Hedge End, Highfield, Hiltingbury, Holbury, Horton Heath, Hythe, Itchen, Lordswood, Maybush, Millbrook, Netley, North Baddesley, Nursling, Otterbourne, Pooksgreen, Romsey, Shawford, Shirley, Swanmore, Swaythling, Totton, Twyford, West End, Wickham etc.

For a complete title listing please visit our website
www.redbooks-maps.co.uk

PORTSMOUTH TO:
JERSEY, GUERNSEY, ST MALO, CAEN,
LE HAVRE, CHERBOURG, BILBAO

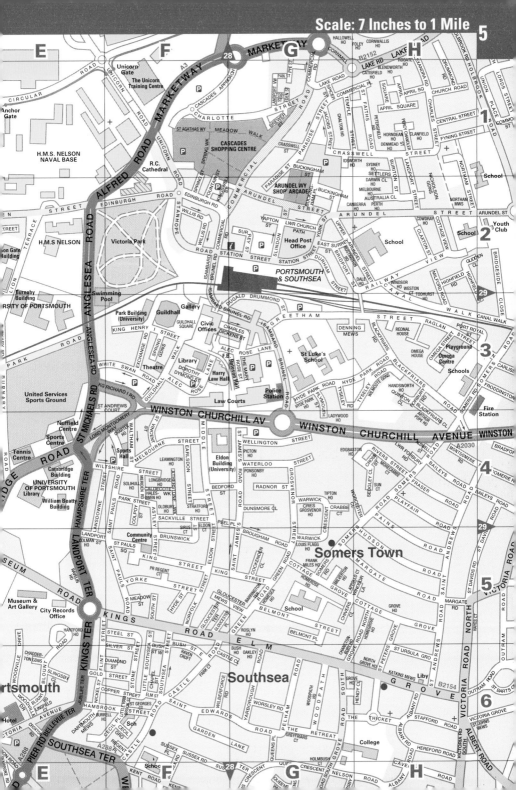

E   F   G   H

MARKETWAY

HALLOWELL FOLEY CORNWALLIS HO
28   CORNHILL   B2152   LAKE RD

Unicorn
Gate
The Unicorn
Training Centre

CATISFIELD   ROGATE STANDARD RD
BLENDWORTH   UNION PLACE

CIRCULAR   ROAD   UNICORN   ROAD

Anchor
Gate

CHARLOTTE

ST AGATHAS WY   MEADOW   WALK

CASCADES
SHOPPING CENTRE

COMMERCIAL   ROAD
LAKE ROAD   SPICER   COMMERCIAL   ROAD

APRIL   SQUARE   CHURCH ROAD

CENTRAL STREET   FYNING STREET

School   1

R.C.
Cathedral

H.M.S. NELSON
NAVAL BASE

ALFRED   ROAD

SPRING   CRASSWELL ST   BUCKINGHAM
ST

PARADISE ST
ARUNDEL WY SHOP ARCADE   Buckingham

CRASSWELL

IDSWORTH
ST   SYDNEY
HO   SETTLERS
DARWIN CL   MELBOURNE   ST
CANBERRA   PERTH
AUSTRALIA CL

EDINBURGH   ROAD

EDINBURGH RD

ANGLESEA   ROAD

STANHOPE   ROAD

WILLIS RD

ARUNDEL   STREET

LWR CHURCH
PATH
YAPTON   ST
SUR   REY
ST   UPPER   ARUNDEL STREET   EAST SURREY

ARUNDEL   STREET

COWDRAY
HO   COTTAGE VIEW
School   2
School   Youth
Club

H.M.S. NELSON

Victoria Park

UNIVERSITY OF PORTSMOUTH

ISAMBARD   BRUNEL RD   COMMERCIAL   ROAD

PARK STATION

PORTSMOUTH
& SOUTHSEA

STATION   STREET
STANHOPE RD

DURHAM   ST
BRIDPORT   ST

RAILWAY   CANAL   WALK

WINDSOR
HO   WESTON
HO   TOADHURST
HO   HIGHFIELD
RD   29

Burnaby
Building

Swimming
Pool

Gallery

ISAMBARD   BRUNEL RD   DUGALD   DRUMMOND ST

GREETHAM   STREET

DENNING
MEWS   PORT ROYAL   RAGLAN STREET
BLACKFRIARS   REDNAL
HOUSE   OMEGA   Playground
Omega
Centre   3
Schools

Park Building
(University)

Guildhall

KING HENRY I   STREET
EXCHANGE ST
SPRING GDNS

GUILDHALL
SQUARE   CHARLES   CHARLES ST
Civic
Offices   DICKENS ST

Theatre

Library

GUILDHALL WALK
ALEC   WALK
DOROTHY
DYMOND   ST   ALEC
ROSE   ROSE   LANE

F.B.
Harry
Law Hall   ROSE   LANE
THE MARY
ROSE   Paterson Hall

St Luke's
School   TYSELEY   HYDE PARK   ROAD
BLACKFRIARS   HANDSWORTH
HO
QUINTON   HO   BLACKFRIARS CL   SOMERS   ROAD   CARLISLE

Fire
Station

Law Courts

Police
Station   HYDE PARK ROAD
HYDE PK   LADYWOOD
HO   POPE   HO

United Services
Sports Ground

ST ANDREWS
COURT   KG RICHARD I RD
WHITE   SWAN   ROAD

WINSTON   CHURCHILL   AV   WINSTON   CHURCHILL   AVENUE   WINSTON

Nuffield
Centre

Sports
Centre

LORD MONTGOMERY   WAY
WALTHAM   ST

VINCENT   ST
MELBOURNE   STREET
EARLSDON   ST

PICTON   ST
JAMES'S ST
WELLINGTON   STREET

EDGBASTON   RIVERS STREET
LWR FORBURY   BAILEYS
BROW   RD   A2030

MONTGOMERIE

Tennis
Centre

Cambridge
Building

Sports
Hall

WILTSHIRE

LEAMINGTON   RD

SOLIHULL
HO   CALDECOTE
HALES-
OWEN HO   WK

Eldon
Building
(University)

WATERLOO   ST
PONSONBY   RD
RADNOR   ST

SERGLEY CL   MOREGREADE
MORECAMBE   RD   SUN   CT

PAINS   ROAD   4   29

William Beatty
Building

UNIVERSITY OF PORTSMOUTH
Library

HAMPSHIRE TER

LANSDOWNE   RD

ST PAULS
ST   PARK STREET   ROAD
COLPOY   ST

STRATFORD
OLDBURY   RD   ST

BEDFORD   ST

DUNSMORE CL

TIPTON
HO   CRABBE
CT   WARWICK
CRES
GROSVENOR
HO

SOMER
FRASER

SOMERSET
ROAD   PLAYFAIR   RD
BAILEYS   ROAD

SOLENT   HO   SACKVILLE   STREET
SIRUS   ST
ELDON   ST   BROUGHAM   ROAD

WARWICK
ST
LOUIS FLAGG
HO

ST ANDREWS   ROAD

Community
Centre

ST PAULS
SQ

PR REGENT   ST
BRUNSWICK

KING   STREET

SAINT   JAMES   STREET
COCKENZEN ST   COTTAGE   GROVE

FRANK
MILES HO
GROVE
HOMEROSE
GROVE   Somers Town

LANDPORT TER

COLMAN   ST

ST PAULS
YORKE   ST
KING   ROAD

HYDE ST
GLOUCESTER
MEWS
VIEW   GLOUCESTER   ROAD

ROSLYN
ST
BELMONT   STREET

CHIVERS
RD   ST PETERS
NORTH
GROVE HO

MARGATE

GROVE   HO   MARGATE
RD   5

Museum &
Art Gallery

City Records
Office

KINGS TER

HARTFORD
HO

STEEL   ST
SILVER   ST
FLINT   ST
GOLD   ST
COPPER   ST

NORFOLK   ST

HAMBROOK   ST

ELM   GROVE

BUSH ST E
CASTLE RD

OAKLEY
RD

ST URSULA GRO
KATKINS MEWS   Liby
B2154

Southsea

WOODVILLE   DRIVE

CHADDER-
TON CONS
SLINGSBY
HO

JUBILEE TER

DIAMOND   ST
STONE   ST
LITTLE SOUTHSEA
ST GEORGES

KINGS ROAD

CASTLE   ROAD

WILBERFORCE   RD

YARBOROUGH   RD
WORSLEY RD

THE   RETREAT

PELHAM   ROAD

WOODPATH   ST PETERS GROVE

THICKET

ALBANY   RD

VICTORIA ROAD NORTH

ST BARTS

Hotel

SOUTHSEA TER

DARTMOUTH
MEWS   CECIL
PL   GRO   ST GEORGES

SUSSEX RD
SUSSEX RD
28   TER

EDWARDS   ROAD

GARDEN   LANE
QUEENS

GREYFRIARS   RD
PELHAM
RD

NELSON   ROAD
ALBANY

HEREFORD ROAD

College

VICTORIA   ROAD   SOUTH

VICTORIA GROVE
ST JOHNS
ROAD

ALBERT   ROAD   6

E   F   G   H

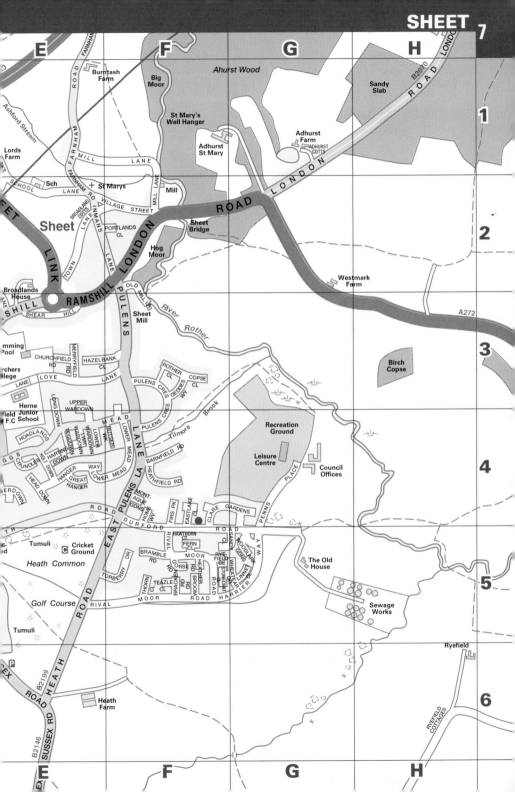

Clanfield

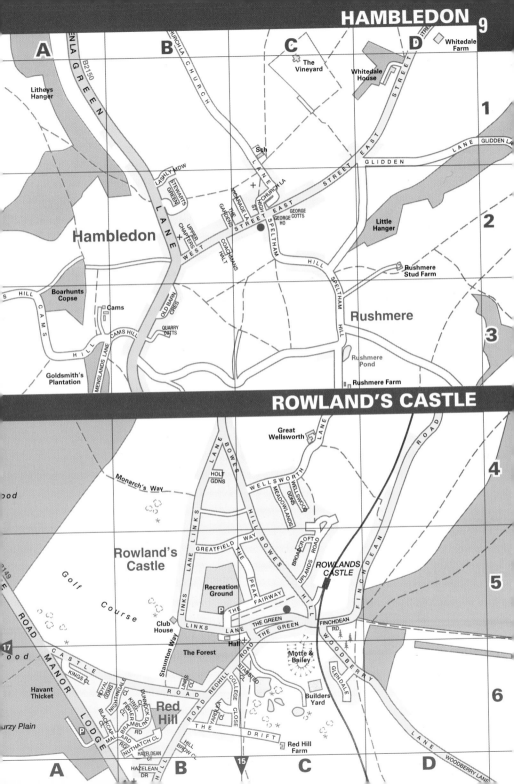

HAMBLEDON

Whitedale Farm

The Vineyard

Whitedale House

Litheys Hanger

Sch

GLIDDEN LANE

GLIDDEN LANE

GLIDDEN

STREET EAST

1

LASHLY MDW

STEWARTS GREEN

THE GARDENS

VICARAGE LANE

CHURCH LA

HIGH STREET

EAST STREET

George Cotts

GEORGE HQ

Little Hanger

2

Hambledon

UPPER CHAPTERS

WEST LANE

CHAPTERS

COACHMANS HALT

SPELTHAM

HILL

SPELTHAM

Rushmere Stud Farm

Boarhunts Copse

Cams

OLD BARN CRES

QUARRY COTTS

CAMS HILL

HILL

Rushmere

3

MERSLANDS LANE

CAMS HILL

Goldsmith's Plantation

Rushmere Pond

Rushmere Farm

ROWLAND'S CASTLE

Great Wellsworth

LANE

ROAD

BOWES LANE

HOLT GDNS

WELLSWORTH

WELLSWOOD GDNS

MEADOWLANDS

4

Monarch's Way

ood

LINKS

HILL

WAY

BOWES

THE

BROADCROFT

FINCHDEAN

Rowland's Castle

GREATFIELD

UPLANDS ROAD

ROWLANDS CASTLE

Golf

LANE LINKS

THE PEAK

HILL

5

0149

Course

Recreation Ground

P

THE FAIRWAY

FINCHDEAN RD

LINKS

Club House

THE GREEN

THE GREEN

WOODBERRY

ROAD

Hall

ROAD MANOR LODGE

CASTLE

Staunton Way

LINKS LANE

The Forest

Motte & Bailey

GLENDALE

6

17

ood

KINGS CL

ROYAL GDNS

NIGHTINGALE CL

Havant Thicket

BLACKCAP RD

KING FISHER

DUNNOCK DR

BRAMBLING

Red Hill

REDHILL ROAD

COLLEGE CLOSE

STANSTED

Builders Yard

LANE

WOODBERRY LANE

urzy Plain

P

MALLARD

NUTHATCH CL

HAZELDEAN

HILL BRDW

THE DRIFT

THE YARDS

Red Hill Farm

HAZELEAN DR

15

| A | B | C | D |

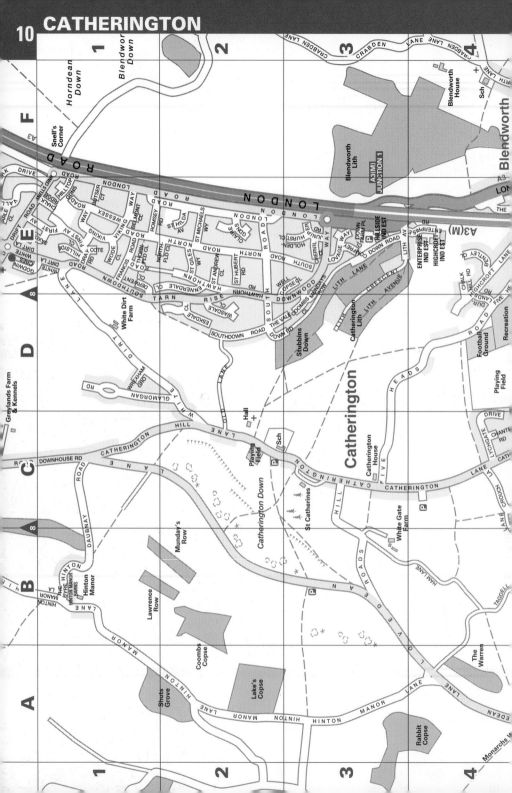

Horndean Down

Blendworth Down

CRABDEN LANE

CRABDEN LANE

CRABDEN LANE

Blendworth House

Sch

Blendworth

Snell's Corner

A3

LONDON ROAD

ROAD

LONDON

ROAD

LONDON

Blendworth Lith

A3(M) JUNCTION 1

A3(M)

A3

LON

THE

Blendworth Lith

LITH LANE

LITH AV

LITH AVENUE

CRESCENT

DOWN ROAD

HILLSIDE IND EST

ENTERPRISE IND EST

HIGHCROFT IND EST

ENTERPRISE

HIGHCROFT RD

CHALK HILL RD

DURRANTS RD

BENTLEY CL

FIVE HEADS

Recreation

DRIVE

WESSEX WAY

VIKING WAY

FIRST AV

HILLSIDE

FIRST AV

CHALK RIDGE

BIDDLE RD

CHALK RIDGE

WELLS CRINK

GLENS

HILLTOP

HILLSIDE RD

ROAD

BUTSER CT

ROMSEY RD

BELMONT CT

CLAIRE GDNS

ST HILDA AV

ST MICHAELS AV

NORTH FLD CL

ST GILES CL

ST ANDREW RD

ST HUBERT RD

NORTH RD

CLAIRE FLD CL

WELL COPSE CL

THE VALE

DOWNWOOD

COOMBS CL

MUNDAYS

HOLDEN HURST CL

DOWN FARM PL

FARM CL

CHERVIL WAY

LOVAGE WAY

DRIFT

WHITE DIRT LA

DIRT LANE

GODWIN CRES

VALE

K

DRIVE

A3

LONDON ROAD

ROAD

LONDON ROAD

CHALK RIDGE

WODE RD

VIKING RD

FRANCIS RD

DENMEAD CL

DEWSDALE CL

HILLSIDE RD

SOUTHDOWN

TARN RISE

HAWTHORN

WASDALE CL

ESKDALE CL

NORTH RD

SOUTH RD

SOUTH RD

DOWN RD

SOUTHDOWN ROAD

White Dirt Farm

WREXHAM GRO

GLAMORGAN RD

WHITE DIRT LANE

WHITE LANE

LANE

Greylands Farm & Kennels

Stubbins Down

Catherington Lith

Football Ground

Playing Field

HEADS

DOWNHOUSE RD

ROAD

CATHERINGTON HILL

LANE

CATHERINGTON DOWN

Hall

Playing Field

Sch

St Catherines

Catherington House

Catherington

CATHERINGTON HILL

FIVE ROADS

CATHERINGTON LANE

LYCHGATE DRIVE

CHANTRY RD

CATH

DAUBNAY

Munday's Row

White Gate Farm

HAM LANE

LANE CROUCH

TAGDELL

ROAD

THE HINTON BYRE

HINTON MANOR BARNS

Hinton Manor

Lawrence Row

HINTON MANOR LANE

FIVE ROADS

LANE

HINTON

HINTON MANOR LANE

LANE

EDEAN

LANE

Coombs Copse

Shuts Grove

Lake's Copse

MANOR

HINTON

Rabbit Copse

Monarchs W

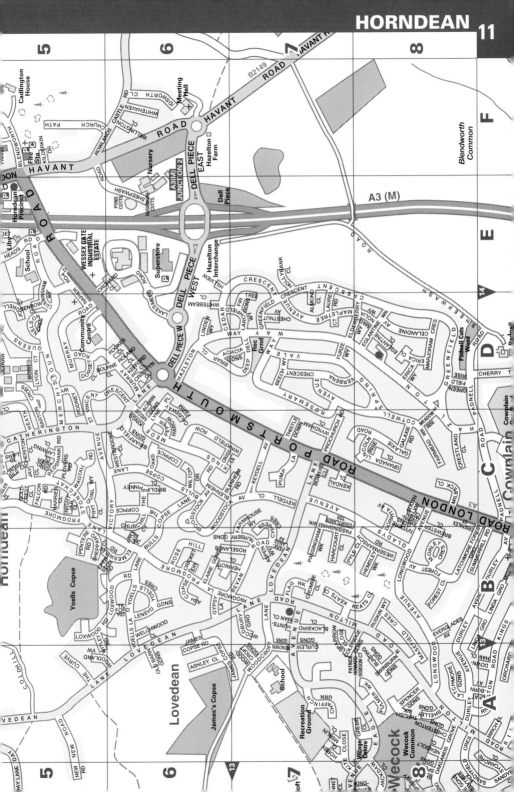

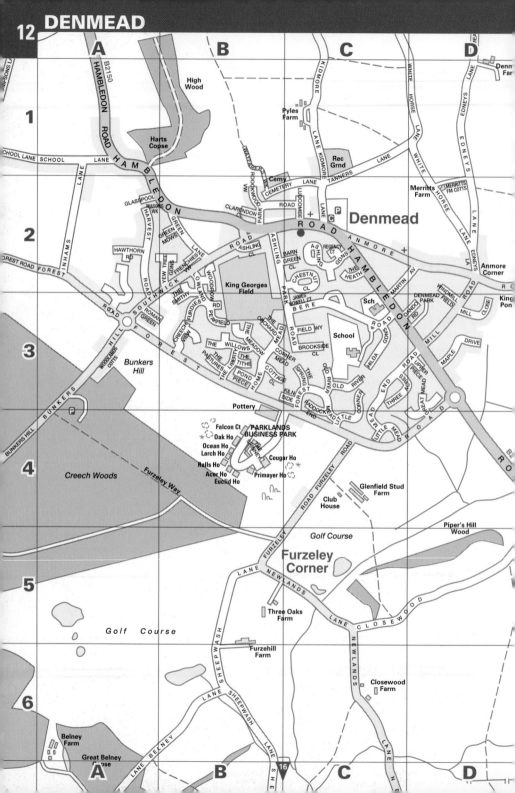

Lovedean

James's Copse

Anmore
Dell

Anmore

Soake

Clarendon
Farm

Woodcroft
Farm

School

Recreation
Ground

Village
Centre

Wecock

Wecock
Common

Park
Woodlands
Centre

Old Park
Farm

THE BRAMBLES
ENTERPRISE PK

THE BRAMBLES
ENTERPRISE PK

Pegasus
Ho

PIPERS WOOD
INDUSTRIAL PARK

STRATHFIELD
PARK

Swimming
Pool

THE
BRAMBLES

BRAMBLES FARM
INDUSTRIAL ESTATE

Tyak Ho

School

Playing Field

School

Park Wood

Recreation
Ground

CHURCHILL YD
IND EST

JUBILEE
BSNS CENTRE

PARKWOOD
CENTRE

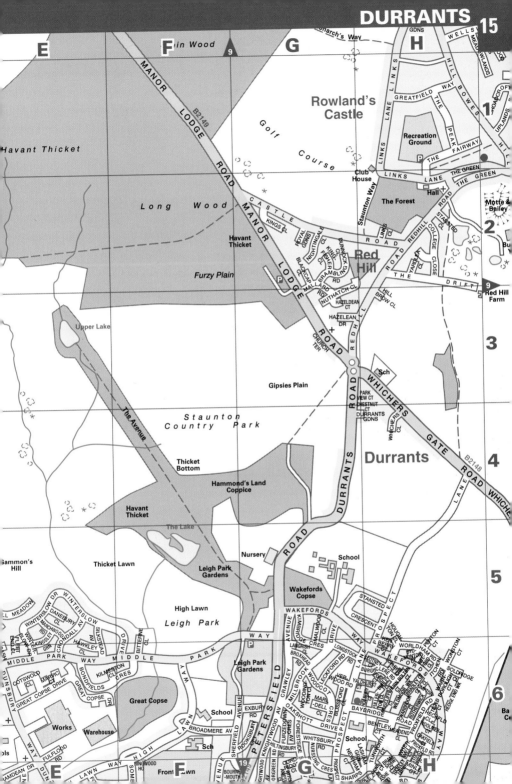

E   **F**   **G**   **H**

in Wood

MANOR LODGE ROAD
B2149

Havant Thicket

Long Wood

Havant Thicket

Furzy Plain

Upper Lake

The Avenue

Staunton Country Park

Thicket Bottom

Hammond's Land Coppice

Havant Thicket

The Lake

Gammon's Hill

Thicket Lawn

High Lawn

Leigh Park

Leigh Park Gardens

Nursery

Wakefords Copse

WAKEFORDS

STANSTED CRESCENT

Winterslow Dr
Danebury Cl
Marchwood
Cl
Winterslow Av
Fleet End Cl
Kingsley Gdn
Kingsley Grn
Cranndall Av
Silkstead Av
Hawkley Cl
Bondfields Cres
Kilmeston Cl
Bittern Cl
Drive

MIDDLE PARK WAY

Cotswold Cl
Marvic Ct
Great Copse Drive
Great Copse

Works

Warehouse

Dunsbury Way

Ringwood Rd

Fulflord Rd

Great Copse

School

Broadmere Av

Leigh Park Gardens

PARK WAY

High Lawn

Sherfield Avenue
Exbury Rd
Rooksbury
Sch

Churchs Way

Rowland's Castle

Golf Course

GDNS
WELLS

LINKS LANE
LINKS LANE

Greatfield Way
The Peak
The Fairway

Hill Bowes

Recreation Ground

Club House

LINKS LANE

Hall

The Forest

Motte & Bailey

CASTLE ROAD

Kings Cl
Royal Gdns
Nightingale Cl
Baker Cl
Bunnock Gdns
King Cl
Blackcap Cl
Brambling Cl
Mallard Rd
Nuthatch Cl
Hazelean Ct
Hazelean Dr
Crouch Ter

Red Hill

The Yardley

College Close

Stansted

Hill Brow Cl

The Drift

Red Hill Farm

Sch
Park View Ct
Chestnut Ct
Durrants Gdns

WHICHERS GATE ROAD
B2148

WHICHERS CLOSE

Durrants

DURRANTS ROAD

School

PROSPECT LANE

WAKEFORD

Staunton Way
Redhill Road

REDHILL ROAD

Gipsies Plain

Leigh Park Gardens

Petersfield Avenue
Crawley Cl
Langrish Cl
Broxhead
Millbrook Cres
Woodcot Cl
Kimbridge Cres
Tedford Rd
Forneth Cl
Yaldhurst Cl
Marl Cl
Dell Cl
Oakshott Dr
Furzedown Cres
Forestside Av
Tilbury Cl
Whitsbury Rd
Nursling Cres
Sharps

Bayridge

School

Kinterbury Rd
Longstock Rd
Worldham Rd
Henton Rd
Finton Rd
Bishopstoke
Wonston Rd
Soldridge Cl
Ringmer Rd
Itchen Rd
Burghclere Rd
Burley Rd
Mislingford Rd
Woolston Rd
Roxford Cl
Weardant
Bentley
Barncroft Way

School

19

BOURNEMOUTH

E   **F**   **G**   **H**

Belney Farm
Belney Copse
A
B
12
C
Lane
D

Sheepwash Farm

Cutlers Farm

Sheepwash Coppice

1

Hazelhook Coppice

Graysland Hummock

Tattle Coppice

Short's Coppice

Ward's Coppice

Dunsland Coppice

2

Lyeheath Farm

Rooks Row

Lye Heath

Fareham Garden

Newlandsmoor Coppice

Newlands Farm

Littlehunts Coppice

Portland Coppice

Cooper Hill

3

Sawyer's Wood

Drivetts Coppice

Greathunts Coppice

PURBROOK

Potwell Coppice

HEATH

Purbrook Heath House

Pond

Broomground Coppice

4

Hookheath Farm

Purbrook Heath Farm

Aldermoor Coppice

Potwell Farm

MILL LANE

WIDLEY WK

ROAD
PURB

Bushy Coppice

Sandy Coppice

5

Mill Farm

Wayfarers Walk

NEW DOWN LANE

Widley Farm

6

Pigeon House Farm

PIGEON HO

A
B
24
C
D

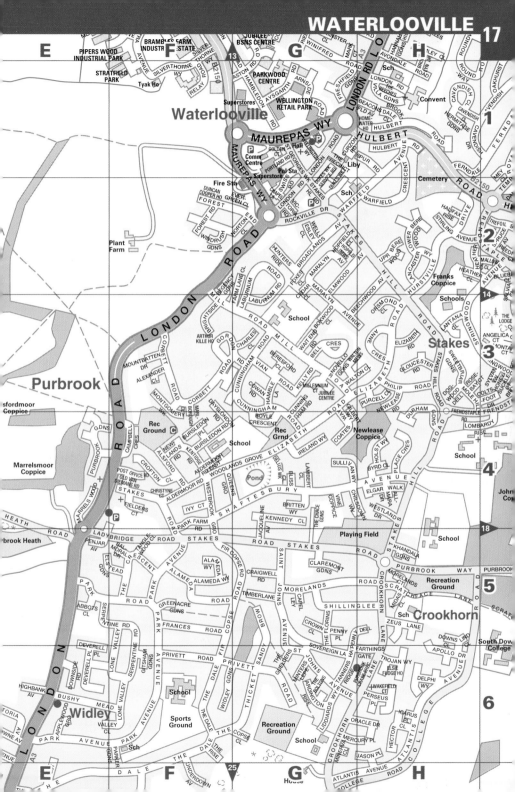

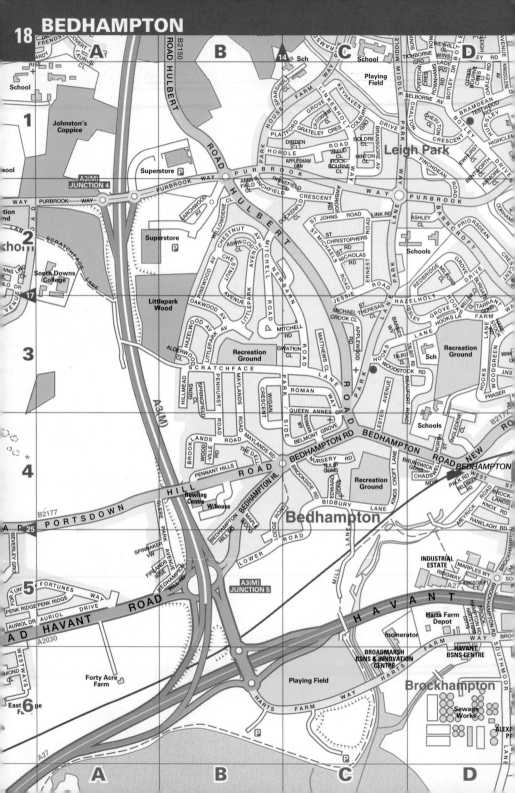

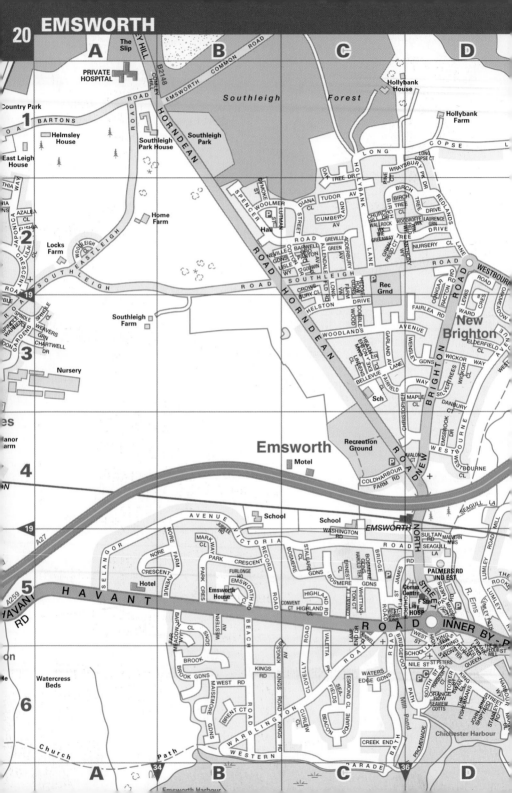

A map of Emsworth with grid references A, B, C, D across the top and numbers 1–6 down the side.

Labels visible on the map include:

The Slip, PRIVATE HOSPITAL, Country Park, BARTONS, Helmsley House, East Leigh House, Locks Farm, WEAVERS GRN, CHARTWELL DR, Nursery, Southleigh Farm, Southleigh Park House, Home Farm, Southleigh Park, Hall, Southleigh, Forest, Hollybank House, Hollybank Farm, LONG COPSE CT, WRAYSBURY PK DR, New Brighton, Rec Grnd, WOODLANDS, Sch, Recreation Ground, Emsworth, Motel, COLDHARBOUR FARM, School, School, WASHINGTON RD, EMSWORTH, SULTAN RD, SEAGULL, PALMERS RD IND EST, Emsworth House, Hotel, Comm Centre, F Stn, Lilly HOSP, Convent CT, Watercress Beds, Kings RD, Waters Edge Gdns, CREEK END, Chichester Harbour, Mill Pond, PROMENADE, Church Path, Emsworth Harbour

Road names include: COMMON ROAD, HORNDEAN ROAD, HAVANT ROAD, SOUTHLEIGH ROAD, SPENCER ROAD, BRIGHTON ROAD, WESTBOURNE, NORTH STREET, INNER BY-P, A27, A259, B2148

E **F** **G** **H**

Foxbury Dell

Didmans Copse

RIVERSIDE COTTS
B2147

Var Cottage Wood

DELL COTTS

WOODMANCOTE

Westbourne

River Ems

School

1

Woodmancote

FOXBURY LANE

WOODMANCOTE LA

CEMETERY LANE

Cemetery

2

DUFFIELD LANE

SOUTH LANE

WALNUT TREE DRI

South Lane Farm

Chantry Farm

Westbourne Court

CHURCH VW

KING ST

FOXBURY RD

NEW ROAD

WHITECHIMNEY ROW

Hall

Hampshire Bridge

Lumley Farm

BROOK COTTS

OLD FARM LANE

SOUTH STEIN LANE

SOUTH LANE

A27

3

MILL LANE

Lumley Mill Farm

SOUTH LANE

HITHER GRN

LAUDER CL

CHESHIRE WY

FRASER GDNS

BREACH

WENTWORTH DR

EAST FIELD CL

4

mley

HASLEMERE RD

ROBIN RD

STEIN RD

BARN FIELD CL

Recreation Ground

Playing Field

Works

KELSEY

GLENWOOD RD

Breach

College

MOUNTWOOD RD

SMALLCUTTS AV

CLOVELLY RD

MERRY CL

KELSEY

FURLONGS

Leisure Centre

ST JOHNS RD

PARK

MANOR GDS

ROMAN CT

HARTLAND

PRIORS CL

COOKS

LANE

MANOR WAY

MANOR GDS

SOUTHBOURNE

Village Hall Liby

GUILDFORD CL

WESTWOOD AV

5

Hermitage

Southbourne

WOODFIELD PARK RD

BRAMLEY GDNS

THISTLEDOWNE GDNS

APPLE GRO

RUSSET GDNS

SOUTHBOURNE AV

LANE

PENNY LANE

TUPPENNY LANE

Caravan Park

Gosden Green

FIRST ROAD

PRINSTED ROAD

SECOND AV

LONGLANDS RD

THE DRIVE

GARSONS RD

TRAFALGAR RD

STEIN RD

LODGEBURY CL

NORTHCOTE GDNS

School

NEW RD

GLEBE HO

MOSDELL RD

GOODWOOD CT

Caravan Site

MAIN

A259

THORNEY ROAD

GORDON ROAD

MILLOY

Gosden Green Nurseries

ROAD

MAIN

ALFREY RD

JUBILEE MEWS

LANGLEY COTTS

HAM LANE

PRINSTED LANE

VICTORIA TER

BARN COTTS

THE SQ

PRINSTED LANE

GARSONS RD

FRARYDENE

THE CRES

CHURCH RD

ROAD

A259

6

Brookside Fruit Farm

Prinsted

E **F** **G** **H**

36

A   B   C   D

1

2

3

4

5

6

A   B   C   D

The Mount

M27

M27

ROAD   JAMES   CA   GHAN

SKEW   ROAD

NELSON   LANE

UPR CORNWAY

LA

DANES

TUDOR
CL

SAXON CL

DORE

MERLIN
GDNS

CORNAWAY AVENUE

LINDEN

REDWOOD

LANCASTER
CL

NORTHFIELD
CL

PARK

CAMP LOT
CRES

HAWTHORN

ROAD

UPR CORNAWAY LA

Gdn of
Remembrance

ELEANORS
WOOD

Crematorium

SEVERN
CL

NHAM

AXON
WK

DRIVE

A27

ROCKINGHAM
WY

PORTCHESTER RD

DORE

THE QUEENS WAY

THE CLOSE

LEDFORD
CL

EXTON
GDNS

KILMISTON

WALTHAM
CL

CAER PERIS VW

WEYHILL

STEEP
CL

ROGATE
GDNS

NYEWOOD

PORTCHESTER
HEIGHTS

HIGH VIEW

ISLAND VW
WK

GRINDLE
CL

JUTE
CL

SOLENT VW

CANONS
BARN CL

RED BARN

ROBINSON
CT

SIMPSON
CL

School

School

HARTING
GDNS

FROXFIELD
GDNS

RISE

RICHMOND

HILL VIEW

LAVEROCK LEA

DORE

HILL

PORTCHESTER

BURITON
CL

ROAD

ANSON

AVENUE

GROVE

BENEDICT
WY

BROWNIN

KEATS

CHAUCER

SHELLEY

DRYDEN

BROWNING AVENUE

EDWARD

SEAVIEW
AV

MORNING-
SIDE AV

RAYMOND

NEWBO

SAUNDERS
HO

JUBILEE

School

PENTLAND RISE   CARLTON

PENTLAND
RISE

LEITH

PORTSVIEW

CONIFER
MEWS

PO
GDNS

PORTSVIEW
GDNS

COLUNTON

SOUTHWICK
AV

MONTROSE
AV

PO
GRO

POBELLO
GRO

AVENUE

MALANION
AV

MALANION

AVENUE

THE
HILLWAY

KELVIN

GROVE

Fire Station

NEW TOWN

NEW
TOWN

GARDEN
CT

MURRILLS
ESTATE

PRIORY CT

NEELANDS
GRO

HOPKINS
CL

PARRY
SULLIVA

School

LEA

HILLWAY   THE

HILLWAY

PORTCHESTER

NEW TOWN

THE CROSSWAY

THE
LEAWAY

PORTSDO

HAMILTON   ROAD

CASTLE
TRADING
ESTATE

Trafal
Wha

Works

CROSSWAY

THE
DOWNSWAY

THE FAIRWAY

THE KINGSWAY

ST HELENA WY

NEWTOWN

JAMES

STATION RD

WEST   STREET   EAST   STREET   SOU

Portcheste

School

Castle Shore
Park

Recreation
Ground

MERROW
CL

RUDGWICK
CRES

STONE
LEIGH CL

HATHERLEY
CRES

QUINTRELL AV

ASH-
STEAD

VUE

HATHERLEY

BRENCHLEY
CL

CRANLEIGH
ROAD

CRANI
CL

SEVERN

GDS

WICOR

ORCHARD

NASSISS

HURST
RD

TATTER-
SHALL
CRES

PATH

The Seagull
P.H.

School

HATHER-
LEY DR

CENTRAL

WHITE

SANDPIT

SEAFIELD
RD

KENYA

KING JOHN
AV

ROAD

AVENUE

WESSEX
GDNS

GROVE

NELSON AVENUE

WHITE-
HAVEN

WESTLANDS

WICOR

MILL

LANE

GROVE

HART

KING JOHN

FOXBURY

CARBERRY

NORGETT WY

CORAL

SEAWAY

DRIVE

CLOSE

Bowling
Green

Tennis
Courts

Community
Centre

ALLENBY
GRO

VINCENT
GRO

FROBISHER
GRO

MARLBOROUGH
GRO

CLIVE GROVE

SHRUBBERY
CL

CHALKY
WALK

WELLINGTON GR

KING GEORGE
RD

ON MAR
RD

SUNNINGDALE   RD

CASTLE

MYRTLE   AVENUE

GROVE

Playing
Field

Sch

Liby

WEST
STREET

JUBILEE

PC

KING GEORGE
RD

ASHETON CT

CASTLE

THE
KEEP

POLSTERN

COWLA

Portcheste

School

BARBICAN
MEWS

WINDSOR

YORK
GDNS

ROAD

MORAUNT
DR

ALBION
CL

AUDRET
CL

WINDMILL

KENT GROVE

COPPINS GRO

COOPER
GRO

ROMAN GROVE

OLIVE
GRO

EDGAR
CRES

HART

WEST
BROOK

NEVICLE
RD

DENVILLE
AV

CASTLE NORMAN
CL

BENHAM
GRO

BAYLY AV

WICOR VIEW ROAD

WICOR PATH

Cemetery

WATER
CASTLE
LEST

Porte
Ce

Spe
Gro

Boat
Yard

Wicor
Lake

HARBOUR
VIEW

MARINA
GRO

GLADSTONE
GDNS

AVENUE

GROVE

ALTON GRO

MERTON CRES

MERTON

GROVE

LANSDOWN AV

LONSDALE AV

BEACHWAY

KENWOOD

KENWOOD
RD

WEBB
RD

ROAD

HOSPITAL   LANE

Pewit
Island

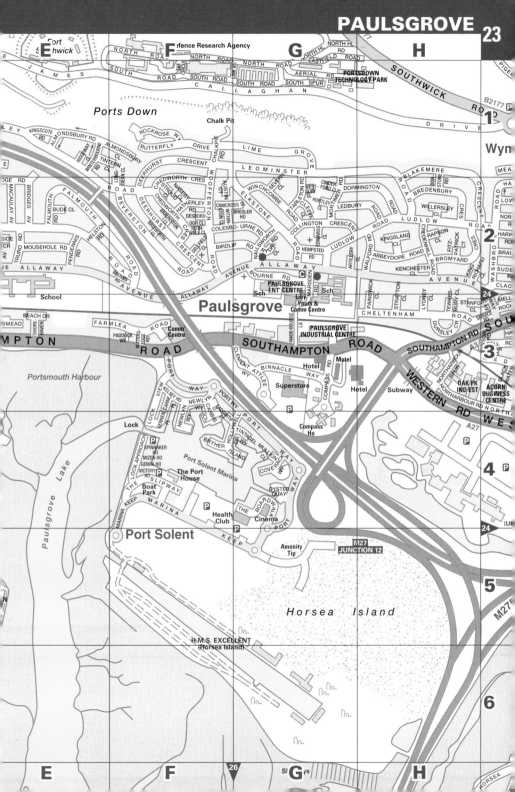

E | F | G | H

Fort S...hwick

Fort E...hwick

Defence Research Agency

NORTH ROAD
NORTH ROAD
THE CIRCUS
NORTH ROAD
NORTH ROAD
NORTH HL RD
NORTH HL RD
EASTFIELD ROAD

SOUTH ROAD
SOUTH ROAD
SOUTH ROAD
SOUTH SPUR
AERIAL RD

CALLAGHAN

PORTSDOWN TECHNOLOGY PARK

SOUTHWICK RD

B2177

Ports Down

DRIVE

Chalk Pit

1

Wyn

ROCKROSE WY
BUTTERFLY DRIVE
CHALKPIT
LIME GROVE
LEOMINSTER

BLAKEMERE ROAD
BREDENBURY
WILLERSLEY

KINGSCOTE RD
ALMONDSBURY RD
ALMONDSBURY CL
DEERHURST CRESCENT
CHEDWORTH CRES
NURSERY CLOUD
HATHERLEY
WINCHCOMBE
SEVERN CL
WEST FORD
CINDER DRI
DORMINGTON
LUDLOW

TINTERN CL
WINTERBOURNE CL
LONG DEAN
CHESTNUT HATHERLEY
CHEDWORTH
BROADSTON
ELKSTONE
STAPLETON RD
HUNTLEY
LEDBURY

RIDGWAY
FALMOUTH
BUDE CL
HELSTON RD
DEERHURST CRESCENT
NASSWORTH RD
DESBORD
ROTH WELL CL
CAMCROSS CL
BRESLER HO
COLLINGTON
MORTIMER
CREDENHILL
RAPSON CL
FITZ-PATRICK CT

2

MOUSEHOLE RD
PENDENNIS RD
BRAVE RD
COLESBO-URNE RD
BIRDLIP RD
NAILSWORTH RD
CLIFFORD
HEMPSTED
WALFORD RD
ABBEYDORE ROAD
KINGSLAND
KENCHESTER CL
BROMYARD
SUDE

School

BEVERSTON ROAD
ALLAWAY AVENUE
ALLAWAY
BOURNE RD
ARTILLERY RD
EDWARDS

PAINSWICK
STRATTON CL
NYTH CL
STANFORD
CLAC

Paulsgrove

PAULSGROVE ENT CENTRE
Sch
Liby, Youth & Comm Centre
Sch

CHELTENHAM

DURSLEY CT

24

SMEAD
BEACH DR
SHORE HAVEN
FARMLEA
PADDOCK WK
WITTERS EDGE RD
Comm Centre

PAULSGROVE INDUSTRIAL CENTRE

SERVICE RD

3

MPTON

ROAD

SOUTHAMPTON ROAD

SOUTHAMPTON RD

WESTERN RD

SOU

Portsmouth Harbour

PORT WAY
VIEW
KELSEY RD
SEINER
CAIRNS
NEWLYN WY
CARBIS
TAGRIMPTON
BINNACLE WY
CLEMENT ATTLEE WY
Hotel
Motel
COMPASS RD

Hotel

Superstore

Subway

OAK PK IND EST
ACORN BUSINESS CENTRE

A27

Lock

Lock

LOCK APPROACH
SPINNAKER HO
MIZEN HO
GENOA HO
VICTORY HO
SLIPWAY
NEWLYN
LOCK VIEW
BRYHER
TINTAGEL HO
ISLAND
MULLION
CL
Compass Ho

4

Paulsgrove Lake

The Port House
Boat Park

Port Solent Marina

MARINA KEEP
THE MARINA
COVER
OYSTER QUAY
THE BOARDWALK
PORT WAY

Health Club

Cinema

Port Solent

Amenity Tip

M27 JUNCTION 12

24

(U)

5

Horsea Island

M27

H.M.S. EXCELLENT
(Horsea Island)

M27

6

E | F | G | H

26

S...rys

HORSEA

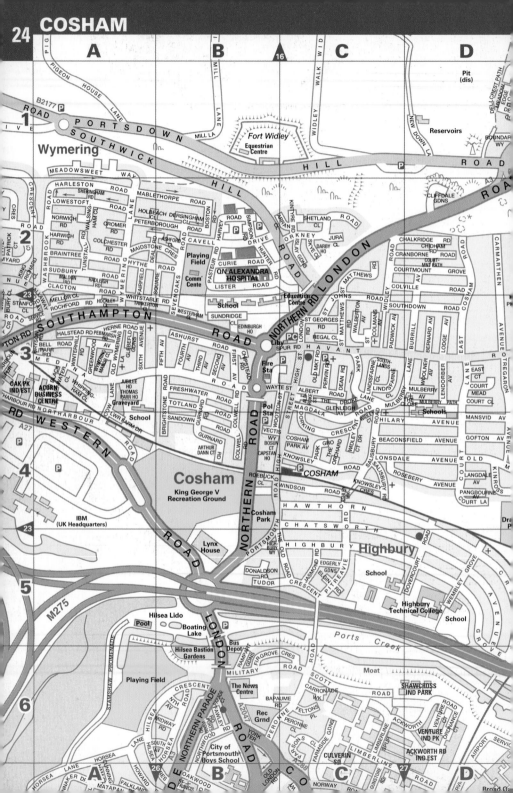

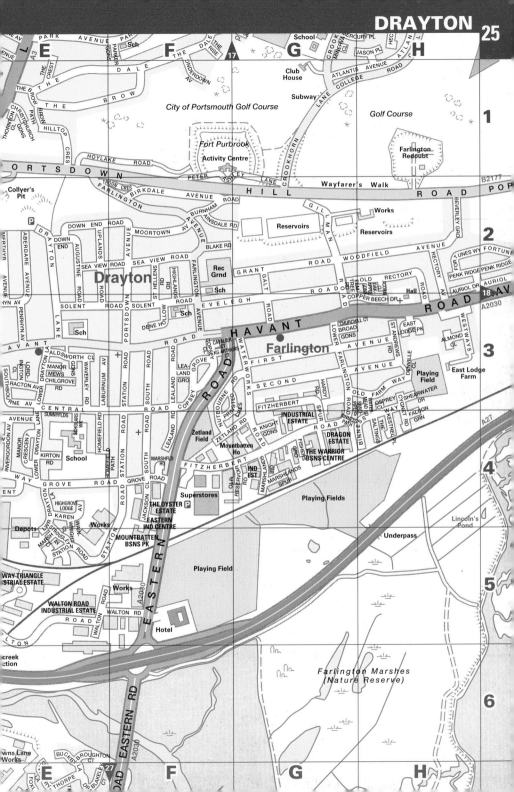

Slipways

Tipner Point

Tipner Lake

Tipner Rifle Range

Brick Kiln Lake

Whale Island

Sports Ground

H.M.S. EXCELLENT (Whale Island)

Stamshaw

Tipner

Greyhound Stadium

Recreation Ground

Leisure Centre

Angling Club

Alexandra Park

Athletics & Cycling Track

Mountbatten Centre

Continental Ferry Port (Vehicular & Freight)

Terminal

Albert Johnson Quay

Landport

H.M. Naval Base

Basin No.3

Flathouse Quay

Rudmore Roundabout

Pol Sta

Victory Ret Pk

Superstores

North E

Comm Centre

City of Portsmo Boys Sch

School

Alexandra Park

Hilsea

Anchorage Park

Copnor

Portsea Island

Baffins

Kingston

Golf Course

Great Salterns Recreation Ground

Great Salterns Lake

Great Salterns Quay

Kingston Cemetery

Frog Lake

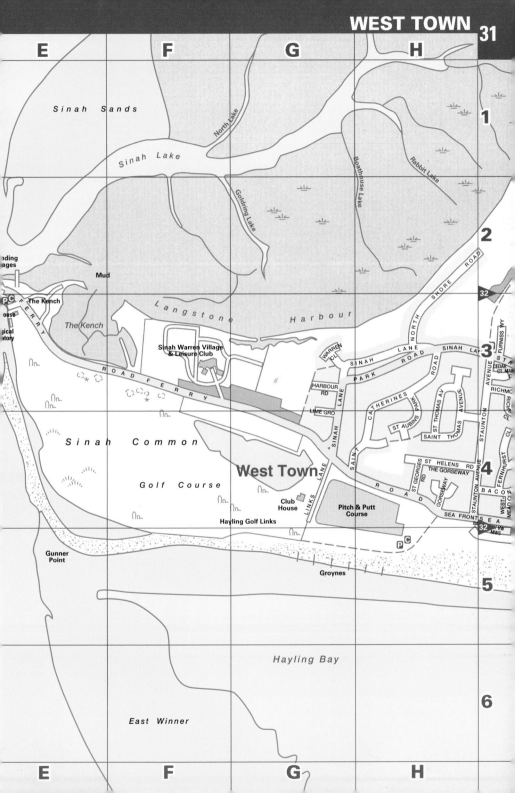

E   F   G   H

1

Sinah Sands

Sinah Lake

North Lake

Golding Lake

Boathouse Lake

Rabbit Lake

2

32

nding ages

Mud

P C

The Kench

ouse

The Kench

jical atory

Langstone   Harbour

FERRY   ROAD

Sinah Warren Village & Leisure Club

WARREN CL

HARBOUR RD

LIME GRO

SINAH LANE

PARK   ROAD

NORTH   SHORE   ROAD

3

FURNISS WY

ST CEDAR CT MA

RICHMC CL

SINAH LANE

SINAH   ROAD

STAUNTON   AVENUE

ROAD   FERRY

Sinah   Common

Golf   Course

West Town

Club House

SAINT   CATHERINES   ROAD

ST AUBINS RD

SAINT THOMAS

ST THOMAS AV

ST THOMAS AVENUE

ST HELENS RD
THE GORSEWAY

ST GEORGES RD

GORSEWAY

STAUNTON AVENUE

WEST FERNHURST CL

BACON

MEADO

4

Hayling Golf Links

LINKS   LANE

SAINT   LEONARDS   ROAD

Pitch & Putt Course

SEA FRONT

SEA

32

VW MWS

Gunner Point

P C

5

Groynes

Hayling   Bay

6

East Winner

E   F   G   H

A B C D

1

2

3

4

5

6

A B C D

Hayling Island

South Hayling

Newtown

Mengham

Westfield

Golf Cour

Golf Centre

Tournerbury Farm

Pound Marsh

Manor House

School

School

School

School

Barn Theatre

Mengham House

Mengham Park

HAVANT ROAD A3023

Honeyrings Copse

The Oven Campsite

Highworth Caravan Park

Hayling Billy Coastal Path

SALTMARSH LANE

WEST LANE

WOODLANDS LA

BRIGHTS LA

HIGWORTH LA

WARDENS

DOVER CL

MANOR RD

GLEBE CL

ATHERLEY RD

ALBERT RD

CHARLESTON CL

DANCES WAY

WEST LANE

NEWTOWN

LYNDEN CL

HAMFIELD DR

AUBREY CL

SYCAMORE DR

FATHOMS

SOUTHLEIGH GRO

BEACH ROAD MANOR ROAD

SAINT MARYS

HILDEN CT

BENWELL CT

Pol Sta

GARDEN CLOSE

HOLLOW LANE

WESTFIELD OAKS AV

ABER ANTHONY

TIMBERS

SOLENT

ST JOHNS

ORCHARD CL

HOLM

VICTORIA

ALEXANDRA AV

TUDOR CL

CHICHESTER AV

MANOR WAY

WEBB

The Sanderlings

WYBORN CL

SEAGROVE AVENUE

GRAND PAR

ORCHARD RD

SEA FRONT ESTATE

NORTH CRES

NORMAN

HAROLD

PEBBLE

OLD SCHOOL

Coastguard Lookout

Amusement Park

Hayling Park Playing Field

Community Centre

STATION AVENUE

FURNISS WY

CEDAR CT

MAPLE CL

RICHMOND DR

FOUNTAIN SQ

JAMES ROAD

RICHMOND CL

STAUNTON AVENUE

THOMAS AVENUE

FERNHURST

LENS

HORSEW

BACON

WEST

FERNMEAD CT

STANFORD RD

STAMFORD AV

JOHNSON

BATHURST CL

FAIRMEAD RD

MAGDALA RD

GREEN LA

LENNOX LODGE

JOHNS RD

NORFOLK MWS

NORFOLK CRES

ANNES

LAUREN MWS

FRONT

SEA

Rook Farm

Gable Head

GABLE MEWS

LEGION RD

Club

Rec' Grnd

Bowling Green

Sch

Fire Sta

Liby

CHURCH ROAD

ST MARYS ROAD

MARYS ROAD

GROVE

ELM GRO

ST LEONARDS AVENUE

WALNUT TREE CL

TREE CL

BRIAR WOOD GDNS

OAKWOOD

ELWELL GRN

ASHWOOD

CHERRYWOOD GDNS

LINCO

FIR TREE

SPENCER

Health Centre

MENGHAM LANE

PALMERSTON RD

CT

ITHICA CL

DUN

DONALD

HERONS CT

GROVE

BURWOOD

POPLAR GRO

BEECH GRO

HAWTHORNE GRO

LABURNUM GROVE

EASTWOOD

TOURNERBURY LANE

MENGHAM AVENUE

SELSMORE AVENUE

MENGHAM RD

ST MARGARETS RD

GOLDRING CL

MY LORDS LA

TEAL RD

OSPREY DR

SWANS WK

SALTER

MENGHAM

GRAND PAR

RAMSEY RD

LYNDHURST RD

RITCHIE RD

BOUND LANE

SCARFF RD

ST ANDREWS CL

ROUNDHOUSE CT

SUNTRAP GDNS

FRONT

Pound Lea

KINGS ROAD

WYLE AV

REST A

LULWORTH CL

KATRINA GDNS

LILAC CL

The Beach

Hayling
Bay

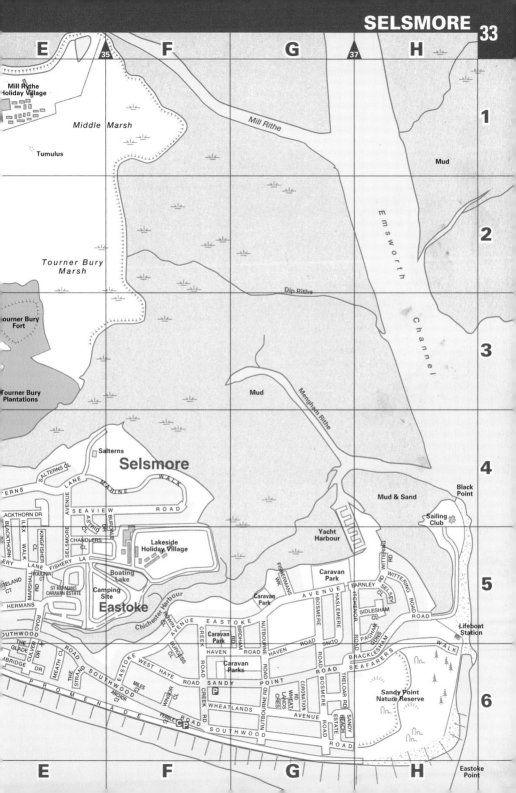

E   35   F   G   37   H

1

Mill Rythe Holiday Village

Middle Marsh

Mill Rithe

Tumulus

Mud

2

Tourner Bury Marsh

Emsworth Channel

Din Rithe

3

Tourner Bury Fort

Mud

Mengham Rithe

Tourner Bury Plantations

Salterns

Selsmore

SALTERNS CL

MARINE

WALK

SEAVIEW

ROAD

BURDALE

ASTRID DR

BLACKTHORN DR

ILEX WALK

BLACKTHORN

KINGFISHER CL

SELSMORE

FISHERY LA

CHANDLERS CL

Lakeside Holiday Village

Yacht Harbour

Mud & Sand

Black Point

Sailing Club

4

TERNS

LANE

AVENUE

SEAVIEW

CL

HOULTON CT

MARSHALL

HELAND CT

Boating Lake

Camping Site

Eastoke

Chichester Harbour

Caravan Park

FISHERMANS WK

Caravan Park

AVENUE

BOSMERE

HASLEMERE

EARNLEY

WITTERING RD

SELSEY

WITTERING ROAD

SIDLESHAM CL

ROAD

Lifeboat Station

5

HERMANS

ST HERMANS CARAVAN ESTATE

ROAD

CULVER DR

SOUTHWOOD

THE GLADE

MBRIDGE DR

MEATH CU

THE STRAND

WINDSOR DR

EASTOKE

ANCHOR CT

MILES CT

ADWIN AVENUE

BURGESS CL

CREEK

ROAD

EASTOKE

HAVEN

Caravan Park

BIRDHAM RD

Caravan Parks

NUTBOURNE RD

POINT

HAVEN

ROAD

GDNS

BOSMERE

ROAD

HASLEMERE

ROAD

PAGHAM

GDNS

ISHENOR RD

TRELOAR RD

BRACKLESHAM

SEAFARERS

WALK

6

THE GLADE

SOUTHWOOD ROAD

WEST HAYE ROAD

SANDY CREEK

WHEATLANDS

PEBBLE CT

CP

SOUTHWOOD

NUTBOURNE RD

CORONATION RD

WHEAT LANDS CRES

BOSMERE AVENUE

SANDY BEACH ESTATE

Sandy Point Nature Reserve

PROMENADE

Eastoke Point

E   F   G   H

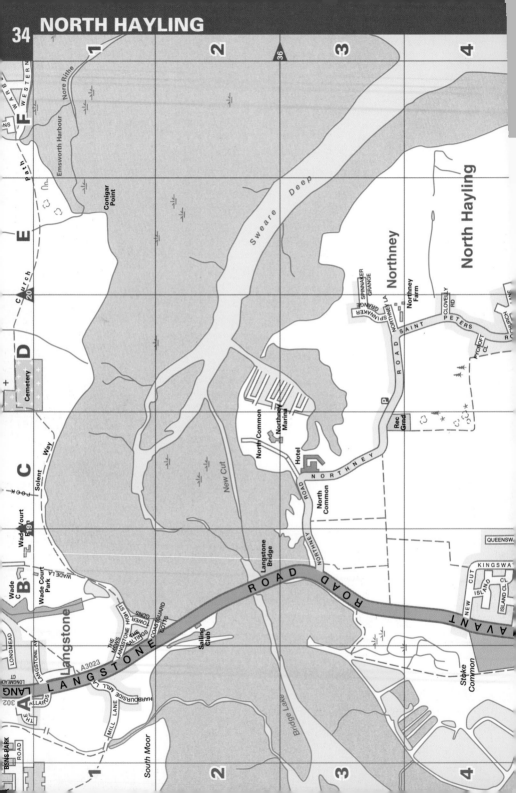

North Hayling

North Hayling

Northney

Northney Farm

SPINNAKER GRANGE

Rec Grnd

Hotel

North Common

Northney Marina

North Common

NORTHNEY

ROAD

R O A D   S A I N T   P E T E R S

PYCROFT CL

CLOVELLY RD

CHURCH LANE

QUEENSW

KINGSWA

ISLAND CL

NEW CUT ISLAND

A V A N T

Langstone Bridge

R O A D   L A N G S T O N E   R O A D

Sailing Club

Langstone

A3023

LONGMEAD CT

LONGMEAD

THE DR

302

TSNS PARK ROAD

THE MEWS

LANGSTONE RD

LANGSTONE HIGH ST

TOWER GDNS

OWEN

SALTINGS

COASTGUARD COTTS

HARBOURSIDE

MILL LANE

ALLARDS

South Moor

Bridge Lake

New Cut

Stoke Common

Sweare Deep

Conigar Point

Emsworth Harbour

Nore Rithe

F WARB WESTERN

NS

Path

Church Path

Cemetery

20

19

Wade Court

Wade Court Park

Wade Ct

WADE LA

Solent Way

Foot Path

36

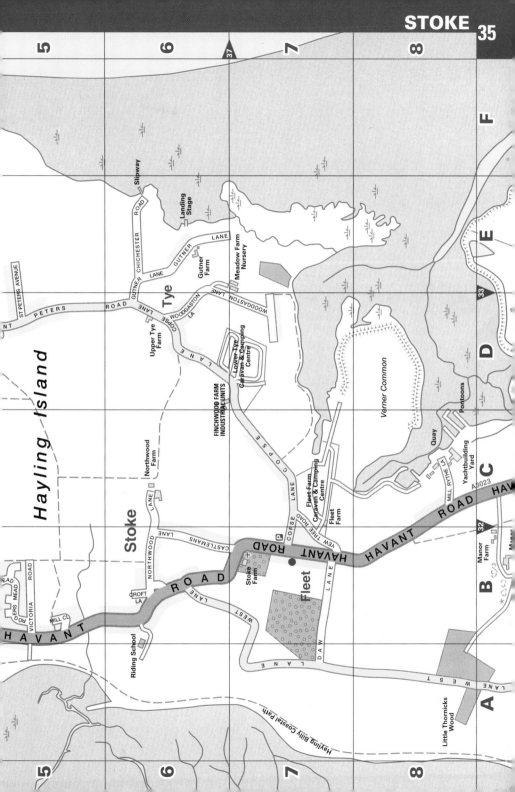

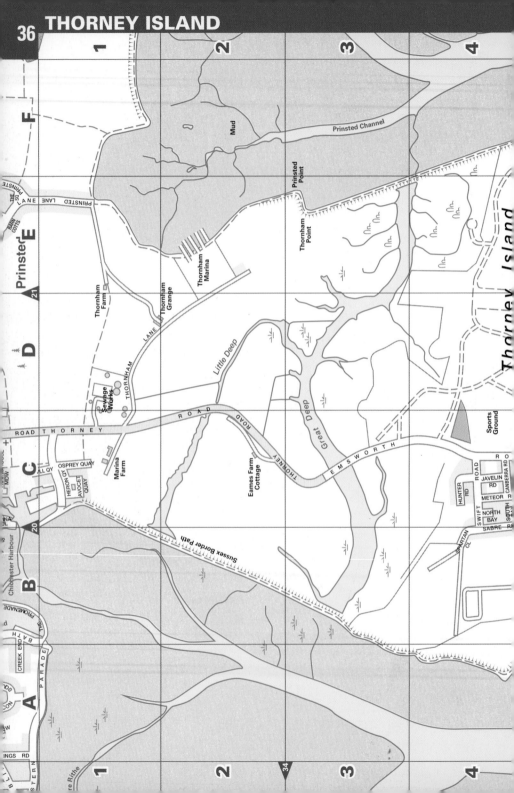

5   6   7   8

F   E   D   C   B   A

Sussex Border Path

West Thorney

AIRFIELD (disused)

Tennis Court

Church Centre

Club

Playground

CHURCH ROAD

VARSITY RD

VICTOR ROAD

VULCAN RD

VALIANT RD

VALETTA RD

SMITH LA

EMSWORTH ROAD

PLEASANT LANE

BAKER BARRACKS

BAKER BARRACKS

WORTH ROAD

EMSWORTH ROAD

Longmere Point

Sussex Border Path

Marker Point

Chichester Harbour

Mud

Emsworth Channel

Point

33

35

The Index includes some names for which there is insufficient space on the maps. These names are indicated by an * and are followed by the nearest adjoining thoroughfare.

A'Becket Ct PO1 4 D5
Abbas Grn*,
Hannington Rd PO9 14 D5
Abbeydore Rd PO6 23 H2
Abbots Cl PO7 17 E5
Abbotstone Av PO9 19 F2
Aberdare Av PO6 25 E2
Acacia Gdns PO8 11 D6
Acer Way PO9 19 H2
Ackworth Rd PO3 24 C6
**Ackworth Rd
Ind Est PO3 24 D6**
**Acorn Bsns
Centre PO6 24 A3**
Acorn Cl PO6 25 H2
Acorn Gdns PO8 11 D6
Acre La PO7 14 C2
Adair Rd PO4 29 H5
Adames Rd PO1 29 F1
Adderbury Av PO10 20 C2
Addison Rd PO4 29 F4
Adhurst Cotts GU31 7 G1
Adhurst Rd PO9 19 F2
Admirals Walk PO1 4 C1
Admiralty Rd PO1 4 C2
Adsdean Cl PO9 18 D2
Adstone La PO3 27 G1
Aerial Rd PO17 23 G1
Agincourt Rd PO2 26 C6
Ainsdale Rd PO6 25 F2
Aintree Dr PO7 14 B2
Airport Service Rd
PO3 27 F1
Airspeed Rd PO3 27 G2
Alameda Rd PO7 17 F5
Alameda Way PO7 17 F5
Albany Rd PO5 5 H6
Albert Gro PO5 29 E4
Albert Rd,
Cosham PO6 24 C3
Albert Rd,
Southsea PO5 5 H6
Albion Cl PO16 22 A5
Albretia Av PO8 13 G3
Alchorne Pl PO3 27 G2
Alderfield GU32 6 B5
Aldermoor Rd PO7 17 F4
Aldermoor Rd East
PO7 17 F4
Alderwood Cl PO9 18 B3
Aldrich Rd PO1 28 C1
Aldridge Cl PO8 8 C3
Aldroke St PO6 24 C3
Aldsworth Cl PO6 25 E3
Aldsworth Gdns PO6 25 E3
Aldwell St PO5 5 H4
Alec Rose La PO1 5 F3
Alex Way PO2 26 C2
Alexander Cl PO7 17 F3
Alexandra Av PO11 32 B5
Alexandra Rd PO1 29 E1
**Alexandria Pk
PO9 18 D6**
Alfred Rd PO1 5 E2
Alfrey Cl PO10 21 G6
Algiers Rd PO3 27 G5
Alhambra Rd PO4 29 F6
All Saints Rd PO1 26 C6
Allaway Av PO6 23 E2
Allbrook Ct PO9 14 D5
Allcot Rd PO3 27 E3
Allenby Gro PO7 22 B3
Allendale Av PO10 20 C2
Allens Rd PO4 29 F5
Allmara Dr PO7 17 H4
Alma Ter PO2 29 H4
**Almeiva Point
PO3 27 G3**
Almond Cl,
Havant PO9 25 H3
Almond Cl,
Waterlooville PO8 11 D7
Almondsbury Cl PO6 23 E1
Almondsbury Rd PO6 23 E1
Alresford Rd PO9 19 E2
Alsford Rd PO7 17 F4

Alten Rd PO7 13 F4
Althorpe Dr PO3 27 G1
Alton Gro PO16 22 B5
Alver Rd PO1 29 F1
Alverstone Rd PO4 29 H2
Amberley Rd,
Portsmouth PO2 26 D2
Amberley Rd,
Waterlooville PO8 8 D3
Amethyst Gro PO7 14 B4
Amey Ind Est GU32 6 B4
Ampfield Cl PO9 18 B2
Amport Ct PO9 14 C6
Amyas Ct PO4 30 B3
Anchor Ct PO11 33 F6
Anchor Gate Rd PO1 4 D1
Anchor La PO1 4 B2
Anchorage Rd PO3 27 G1
Anderson Cl PO9 19 G3
Andover Rd PO4 29 G5
Andrew Bell St PO1 28 D1
Andrew Cl PO3 29 G1
Andrew Cres PO7 13 F5
Angelica Cl PO7 14 A6
Angelo Cl PO7 14 A4
Angerstein Rd PO2 26 C4
Anglesea Rd PO1 5 E3
Anmore Cl PO9 18 D2
Anmore Dr PO7 13 F4
Anmore Rd PO7 12 C2
Anne Cres PO7 17 H3
Annes Ct PO11 32 A5
Anson Cl PO1 4 C4
Anson Gro PO16 22 C1
Anson Rd PO14 29 G2
Anthony Way PO10 20 C2
Anvil Cl PO7 14 C2
Apollo Dr PO7 17 H6
Apple Gro PO10 21 E5
Applegate Pl PO8 11 B6
Appleshaw Grn PO9 18 C1
Applewood Gro PO7 17 E6
Applewood Rd PO9 18 C3
Appollo Ct PO5 5 G5
April Sq PO1 5 H1
Apsley Rd PO4 29 H3
Ardington Rise PO7 17 G6
Arethusa Ho PO1 4 C4
Ariel Rd PO1 29 F2
Arle Cl PO8 8 D4
Armory La PO1 4 D4
Armstrong Cl PO7 13 F5
Arnaud Cl PO2 26 C5
Arnside Rd PO7 17 G1
Arragon Ct PO7 14 A4
Arran Cl PO6 24 B2
Arthur Dann Ct PO6 24 B4
Arthur Kille Ho PO7 17 F3
Arthur Pope Ho PO5 5 H4
Artillery Cl PO6 23 G2
Arun Cl GU32 6 C6
Arundel St PO1 5 G2
**Arundel Way Shopping
Arc PO1 5 G2**
Ascot Rd PO3 27 F6
Ash Cl PO8 13 G4
Ash Copse PO8 11 B6
Ashburton Rd PO6 28 D5
Ashby Pl PO5 28 D5
Ashe Rd PO9 19 H1
Ashford Cl PO6 24 B2
Ashington Cl PO8 11 C8
Ashlett Lawn PO9 14 C6
Ashley Cl,
Havant PO9 18 D2
Ashley Cl,
Waterlooville PO8 11 A6
Ashley Walk PO6 24 C4
Ashling Cl PO7 12 B2
Ashling Gdns PO7 12 C2
Ashling La PO2 26 C4
Ashling Park Rd PO7 12 B2
Ashurst Rd PO6 24 B3
Ashwood Cl,
Havant PO9 18 B2
Ashwood Cl,
Hayling Island PO11 32 C4
Aspen Way PO8 11 B7
Assheton Cl PO16 22 C3
Astley St PO5 5 F4
Aston Rd,
Southsea PO4 29 G4
Aston Rd,
Waterlooville PO7 17 G1

Astrid Cl PO11 33 E4
Atalanta Cl PO4 30 B2
Atherley Rd PO11 32 A2
Atherstone Walk PO5 5 F4
Atlantis Av PO7 25 G1
Aubrey Cl PO11 32 A3
Auckland Rd East
PO5 28 D5
Auckland Rd West
PO5 28 D5
Audret Cl PO16 22 C5
Augustine Rd PO6 25 E2
Auriol Dr PO9 25 H3
Austin Ct PO6 23 F2
Australia Cl PO1 5 H2
Avalon Ct PO10 20 D4
Avenue De Caen PO5 28 D6
Avenue Rd PO1 34 B4
Avington Gdns*,
Worldham Rd PO9 14 D6
Avocet Cl PO4 30 A5
Avocet Quay PO10 36 C1
Avocet Way PO8 10 C4
Avon Cl GU32 6 B6
Avondale Cl,
Portsmouth PO1 26 D6
Avondale Rd,
Waterlooville PO7 13 H6
Awbridge Rd PO9 18 C2
Aylen Rd PO3 27 F3
Aylesbury Rd PO2 27 E5
Aylward St PO1 4 D2
Aysgarth Rd PO7 17 G1
Azalea Cl PO9 19 F1

Badger Brow PO7 14 A5
Baffins Rd PO3 29 H1
Baileys Rd PO5 5 H4
Baker St PO1 26 C6
Balchin Ho PO1 4 D2
Balderton Cl PO2 26 D1
Balfour Rd PO2 26 D3
Balliol Rd PO2 26 D3
Balmoral Dr PO7 17 F5
Balmoral Way GU32 6 C3
Bamford Ho PO4 30 A5
Bannerman Rd GU32 6 C3
Bapaume Rd PO3 24 B6
Barbican Mews PO16 22 D4
Barentin Way GU31 6 D3
Barham Rd GU32 6 C4
Barn Cl PO10 20 B5
Barn Cotts PO10 21 G6
Barn Fold PO7 14 B2
Barn Green Cl PO7 12 C2
Barncroft Way PO9 18 D2
Barnes Rd PO1 29 F1
Barnes Way PO9 18 C3
Barney Evans Cres
PO8 13 G4
Barnfield Cl PO10 21 H4
Barnfield Rd GU31 7 F4
Barrington Ter PO5 5 G5
Barton Cross PO8 11 C5
Barton Gro PO3 27 G1
Bartons Rd PO9 19 G1
Barwell Gro PO10 20 C2
Basin St PO2 26 C4
Basing Rd PO9 19 E1
Bassett Walk PO9 14 D5
Bath Rd,
Emsworth PO10 20 C6
Bath Rd,
Southsea PO4 29 G4
Bath Sq PO1 4 B5
Bathing La PO1 4 B5
Bathurst Cl PO11 32 A4
Bathurst Way PO2 26 A3
Battenburg Av PO2 26 D2
Battens Way PO9 19 F1
Battery Row PO1 4 C6
Bay View Cl PO11 31 H4
Bay View Mews PO11 32 B4
Baybridge Rd PO9 15 G6
Bayly Av PO16 22 C6
Baythorn Cl PO2 26 C6
Beach Dr PO6 23 G3
Beach Rd,
Emsworth PO10 20 B5
Beach Rd,
Hayling Island PO11 32 B4
Beach Rd,
Southsea PO5 29 E6

Beachway PO16 22 C5
Beacon Sq PO10 20 C6
Beaconsfield Av,
Portsmouth PO6 24 C4
Beaconsfield Av,
Waterlooville PO7 17 H1
Beasant Cl PO3 30 A1
Beatrice Rd PO4 29 F5
Beaufort Rd,
Havant PO9 18 C3
Beaufort Rd,
Southsea PO5 29 E6
Beaulieu Av PO9 14 D6
Beaulieu Rd PO2 26 D4
Beck St PO1 5 E2
Beckham La GU32 6 B3
Bedford Cl PO9 19 G5
Bedford Rd GU32 6 B5
Bedford St PO5 5 F4
Bedhampton Hill PO9 18 B4
Bedhampton Hill Rd
PO9 18 B5
Bedhampton Rd,
Havant PO9 18 C4
Bedhampton Rd,
Portsmouth PO2 27 E4
Bedhampton Way
PO9 19 E1
Beech Cl PO8 13 H5
Beech Gro PO11 32 D3
Beech Rd PO8 8 C3
Beech Way PO8 11 D7
Beecham Rd PO1 26 D6
Beechwood Av PO7 17 G3
Beechwood Rd PO2 26 D1
Beechworth Rd PO9 19 F5
Beehive Walk PO1 4 D4
Belgravia Rd PO2 27 E4
Bell Cres PO7 17 G3
Bell Hill GU32 6 B1
Bell Hill Ridge GU32 6 B2
Bell Rd PO6 24 A3
Bellair Rd PO9 19 G5
Bellevue La PO10 20 C3
Bellevue Ter PO5 5 E6
Bellinger Ho PO9 18 D4
Belmont Cl PO8 10 E1
Belmont Gro PO9 18 C4
Belmont Pl PO5 5 G5
Belmont St PO5 5 G5
Belmore Cl PO1 26 D6
Belney La PO17 16 A1
Belvedere Cl GU32 6 C3
Bembridge Cres PO4 29 F6
Bembridge Dr PO11 33 E6
Benbow Cl PO8 11 D5
Benbow Ho PO1 4 C2
Benbow Pl PO1 4 C2
Benedict Way PO16 22 D1
Beneficial St PO1 4 C2
Benham Dr PO3 27 E1
Benham Gro PO16 22 C5
Bentley Cl PO8 10 E4
Bentley Ct PO8 15 H6
Bentworth Cl PO9 18 D2
Bepton Down GU31 6 D4
Bere Rd PO7 12 C3
Beresford Cl PO7 17 G3
Beresford Rd PO2 26 D3
Berkeley Sq PO9 19 G5
Berkshire Cl PO1 29 E2
Bernard Av PO6 24 D3
Berney Rd PO4 30 A3
Bernina Av PO7 13 F5
Bernina Cl PO7 13 F5
Berrydown Rd PO9 14 C5
Bertie Rd PO4 30 A3
Bettesworth Rd PO1 26 D6
Betula Cl PO7 14 A6
Bevan Cl PO8 11 B7
Beverley Gro PO4 25 H2
Beverston Rd PO6 23 F2
Bevis Rd PO2 26 C4
Bickton Walk PO9 14 D5
Bidbury La PO9 18 C4
Bill Stilwell Ct*,
Winstanley Rd PO2 26 B3
Billett Av PO7 13 H6
Billing Cl PO4 29 H4
Billy Lawn Av PO9 19 F1
**Bilton Bsns Pk
PO3 27 H3**
Bilton Way PO3 27 H2

Binnacle Way PO6 23 G3
Binness Path PO6 25 G4
Binness Way PO6 25 H4
Binsteed Rd PO2 26 D5
Birch Cl PO8 13 G4
Birch Tree Cl PO10 20 C2
Birch Tree Dr PO10 20 C2
Birdham Rd PO11 33 G5
Birdlip Cl PO8 11 C6
Birdlip Rd PO6 23 F2
Birkdale Av PO6 25 F2
Bishop St PO1 4 D2
Bishopstoke Rd PO9 18 E1
Bitterne Cl PO9 18 D4
Blackberry Cl PO8 8 D4
Blackbird Cl PO8 11 B7
Blackcap Cl PO9 9 A6
Blackdown Cres PO9 19 E2
Blackfriars Cl PO5 5 H3
Blackfriars Rd PO5 5 H3
Blackmoor Walk*,
Baybridge Rd PO9 15 H6
Blackthorn Dr PO11 33 E4
Blackthorn Rd PO11 33 E4
Blackthorn Ter PO1 4 D1
Blackthorn Walk PO7 14 B2
Blackwater Cl PO6 24 A3
Bladon Cl PO9 19 H3
Blake Ho PO1 4 C4
Blake Rd PO9 25 F2
Blakeley Ct PO3 27 H1
Blakemere Cres PO6 23 H2
Blendworth Cres PO9 19 E2
Blendworth Ho PO1 5 H1
Blendworth La PO8 11 F5
Blendworth Rd PO4 29 H2
Blenheim Cl PO4 29 H4
Blenheim Gdns PO9 19 H3
Blenheim Rd PO8 11 C6
Bliss Cl PO7 17 G4
Blissford Cl PO9 15 G6
Blossom Sq PO1 4 D1
Blount Rd PO1 5 E6
Bluebell Cl PO7 14 A5
Blueprint Portfield Rd
PO3 27 F3
Boarhunt Cl PO1 29 E1
Bodmin Rd PO6 23 F2
Bolde Cl PO3 27 F2
Boldre Cl PO9 18 C1
Bonchurch Rd PO4 29 H2
Bondfields Cres PO9 15 E6
Bonfire Cnr PO1 4 C1
Bordon Rd PO9 19 E1
Borough Gro GU32 6 B5
Borough Rd GU32 6 B5
Bosham Rd PO2 27 E5
Bosmere Gdns PO10 20 C5
Bosmere Rd PO11 33 G5
Boston Rd PO6 24 B2
Bosun Ct PO6 24 B4
Botley Dr PO9 18 D1
Boulton Rd PO5 29 F4
Bound La PO11 32 C5
Boundary Way,
Havant PO9 19 E4
Boundary Way,
Portsmouth PO6 24 D1
Bourne Cl PO8 11 D5
Bourne Rd PO6 23 G2
Bourne View Cl PO10 21 G4
Bournemouth Ho PO9 19 F1
Bowen La GU31 6 D7
Bowers Cl PO8 11 C7
Bowes Hill PO9 9 B4
Bowes-Lyon Ct PO8 11 D5
Bowler Av PO3 27 E6
Bowler Ct PO3 27 E6
Boxwood Cl,
Fareham PO16 22 A2
Boxwood Cl,
Waterlooville PO7 17 G3
Boyle Cres PO7 17 G4
Bracken Heath PO7 14 B3
Bracken Rd GU31 7 F5
Bracklesham Rd PO11 33 G6
Bradford Rd PO5 5 H4
Brading Av PO4 29 H5
Bradley Cl PO9 15 H6
Braemar Av PO6 24 D4
Braintree Rd PO6 24 A2
Braishfield Rd PO9 19 F2
Bramble Cl PO7 19 H3
Bramble La PO8 8 B2

Bramble Rd, Petersfield GU31   7 F5
Bramble Rd, Southsea PO4   29 F3
Brambles Fm Ind Est PO7   13 F6
Brambling Rd PO9   9 B6
Bramdean Dr PO9   18 D1
Bramley Cl PO7   13 H6
Bramley Gdns PO10   27 G1
Brampton La PO3   27 G1
Bramshaw Ct PO9   19 H1
Bramshott Rd PO4   29 G3
Brandon Rd PO5   29 E5
Bransbury Rd PO4   30 A4
Bransgore Av PO9   18 C1
Brasted Ct PO4   30 A2
Braunston Cl PO9   23 F2
Braxall Lawn PO9   14 D6
Breach Av PO10   21 G4
Brecon Av PO6   24 D2
Brecon Ho PO1   4 C4
Bredenbury Cres PO6   23 H2
Breech Cl PO3   27 E1
Brenchley Cl PO16   22 A3
Brent Ct PO10   20 B6
Bresler Ho PO6   23 G2
Brewer St PO1   5 G1
Brewster Cl PO8   11 B8
Briar Cl PO8   11 D6
Briarfield Gdns PO8   11 C6
Briarwood Gdns PO11   32 A2
Bridefield Cl PO8   13 F4
Bridefield Cres PO8   13 F4
Bridge Rd PO10   20 C5
Bridgefoot Path PO10   20 C5
Bridges Av PO6   23 E2
Bridgeside Cl PO1   29 E2
Bridget Cl PO8   11 E5
Bridport St PO1   5 G2
Brigham Cl PO2   26 D2
Brights La PO11   32 B2
Brightside PO7   17 F3
Brightstone Rd PO6   24 B4
Bristol Rd PO4   29 G5
Britain St PO1   4 D3
Britannia Rd PO5   29 E3
Britannia Rd North PO5   29 E3
Britannia St GU31   6 D3
Britten Way PO7   17 G4
Brixworth Cl PO16   23 F2
Broad Gdns PO6   25 G3
Broad St PO1   4 B5
Broadcroft PO9   9 C5
Broadland Cotts GU32   7 E2
Broadlands Av PO7   17 G2
Broadmarsh Bsns & Innovation Centre PO9   18 C6
Broadmeadows La PO7   14 A4
Broadmere Av PO9   15 F6
Broadway La PO8   13 F1
Brockenhurst Av PO9   19 E5
Brockhampton Rd PO9   18 D5
Brocklands PO9   18 D4
Brompton Rd PO4   29 G5
Bromyard Cres PO6   23 H2
Brook Cotts PO10   21 E3
Brook Gdns PO10   20 B6
Brookdale Cl PO7   17 H1
Brookfield Cl PO9   19 E3
Brookfield Rd PO1   29 F1
Brooklands Rd PO8   18 B4
Brooklyn Dr PO7   17 H1
Brookmead Way PO9   19 E6
Brookside Cl PO7   12 C3
Brookside Rd, Bedhampton PO9   18 C4
Brookside Rd, Brockhampton PO9   18 D5
Broom Cl, Southsea PO4   30 C3
Broom Cl, Waterlooville PO7   14 A6
Broom Rd GU31   7 F5
Broom Sq PO4   30 C2
Brougham Rd PO5   5 G5
Broughton Ct PO3   25 E6
Brow Path PO7   25 E1
Browning Av PO6   22 D1
Brownlow Cl PO1   26 D2
Broxhead Rd PO9   15 G6
Bruce Rd PO4   29 G5
Brunel Rd PO2   26 D2
Brunswick Gdns PO9   18 C4

Brunswick St PO5   5 F5
Bryher Island PO6   23 F4
Bryony Way PO7   14 A5
Bryson Rd PO6   24 A3
Buckby La PO3   25 E6
Buckingham Pl PO1   5 H2
Buckingham Rd GU32   6 B4
Buckingham St PO1   5 G1
Buckland Cl PO7   13 F4
Buckland Path PO2   26 C6
Buckland St PO2   26 D6
Bucklers Ct, Havant PO9   14 D4
Bucklers Ct, Portsmouth PO2   26 C4
Buckmore Av GU32   6 B3
Bude Cl PO6   23 E2
Bulbeck Rd PO9   19 E5
Bulls Copse La PO8   11 B6
Bulmer Ho GU31   6 D3
Bunkers Hill PO7   12 A4
Bunting Gdns PO8   11 A8
Burbidge Gro PO4   29 G5
Burcote Dr PO3   27 G1
Burdale Dr PO11   33 F4
Burgate Cl PO9   18 D2
Burgess Cl PO11   33 F6
Burghclere Rd PO9   15 G6
Burgoyne Rd PO5   29 E6
Burgundy Ter PO2   26 D2
Buriton Cl PO16   22 C2
Buriton St PO1   5 H1
Burleigh Rd PO1   26 D5
Burley Cl PO9   15 H6
Burlington Rd PO2   26 D4
Burnaby Rd PO1   5 E3
Burnham Rd PO6   25 F2
Burnside PO7   14 A3
Burrell Ho PO5   5 E6
Burrfields Rd PO3   27 E4
Burrill Av PO6   24 D3
Burrows Ct PO9   19 G3
Bursledon Pl PO7   17 F4
Bursledon Rd PO7   17 F4
Burwood Gro PO11   32 C2
Bush Ho PO5   5 G6
Bush St East PO5   5 F6
Bush St West PO5   5 F6
Bushy Mead PO7   17 E6
Butcher St PO1   4 C3
Butser Cl PO8   10 E1
Butser Walk GU31   7 F4
Butterfly Dr PO6   23 F1
Byden Ct PO8   8 D1
Byerley Cl PO10   21 E1
Byerley Rd PO1   29 G2
Byrd Cl PO7   17 H4
Byron Rd PO2   26 C5

Cadgwith Pl PO6   23 F3
Cadnam Lawn PO9   14 D5
Cadnam Rd PO4   30 A4
Cador Dr PO16   22 A4
Caer Peris Vw PO16   22 B1
Cairo Ter PO2   26 C6
Caldecote Walk PO5   5 F4
Calder Ho PO1   4 C2
Calshot Rd PO9   14 C5
Camber Pl PO1   4 C6
Cambridge Rd PO1   5 E6
Camcross Cl PO6   23 F2
Camelia Cl PO9   19 H2
Camelot Cres PO16   22 A2
Campbell Cres PO7   17 F4
Campbell Rd PO5   29 E4
Campion Cl PO7   14 A6
Cams Hill PO1   9 A3
Canal Walk PO1   5 H2
Canberra Ho PO1   5 G2
Canberra Rd PO10   36 C4
Canons Barn Cl PO16   22 B2
Canterbury Rd PO4   29 G4
Capel Ley PO7   17 G5
Capstan Ho PO6   24 B4
Captains Row PO1   4 C5
Carberry Dr PO16   22 A4
Carbery Ct PO9   14 D5
Carbis Cl PO6   23 F3
Cardiff Rd PO2   26 C3
Cardinal Dr PO7   14 B3
Carisbrooke Cl PO9   19 H4
Carisbrooke Rd PO4   29 G3
Carlisle Rd PO6   29 E2
Carlton Rd PO16   22 C1
Carmarthen Av PO6   24 D2
Carnarvon Rd PO2   27 E5
Carne Pl PO6   23 F3
Caroline Lodge PO1   4 D1
Carpenter Cl PO4   29 H4
Carronade Walk PO3   24 C6

Carshalton Av PO6   24 D3
Cascades App PO1   5 F1
Cascades Shopping Centre PO1   5 F1
Castle Av PO9   19 H5
Castle Cl PO5   5 F6
Castle Gdns GU32   6 C4
Castle Gro PO16   22 C4
Castle Rd, Rowlands Castle PO9   9 A6
Castle Rd, Southsea PO5   5 F6
Castle St PO16   22 C3
Castle Trading Est PO16   22 D3
Castle View Rd PO16   22 C1
Castle Way PO9   19 H5
Castlemans La PO11   35 B6
Cathedral Ho PO1   4 C5
Catherington Hill PO8   10 C1
Catherington La PO8   10 C3
Catherington Way PO9   19 E2
Catisfield Ho PO1   5 H1
Catisfield Rd PO4   29 H2
Causeway Fm PO8   11 C6
Cavalier Ct PO9   25 F3
Cavell Dr PO6   24 B2
Cavendish Ct PO7   17 H1
Cavendish Dr PO7   17 H1
Cavendish Rd PO5   29 E4
Cecil Gro PO5   5 F6
Cecil Pl PO5   5 F6
Cedar Cl PO7   17 G3
Cedar Cres PO8   11 D6
Cedar Ct PO11   32 A3
Cedar Gdns PO9   19 G3
Cedar Gro PO3   27 G6
Celandine Av PO8   11 D8
Celia Cl PO7   14 B3
Cemetery La, Emsworth PO10   21 F2
Cemetery La, Waterlooville PO7   12 B2
Centaur St PO2   26 C5
Centenary Gdns PO9   19 E4
Central Point PO3   30 A1
Central Rd, Fareham PO16   22 A3
Central Rd, Portsmouth PO6   25 E3
Central Sq PO1   4 C3
Central St PO1   5 H1
Centurin Ct PO1   4 C4
Centurion Gate PO4   30 B4
Chadderton Gdns PO1   5 H1
Chadswell Mdw PO9   18 D4
Chaffinch Grn PO8   11 A7
Chalk Hill Rd PO8   10 E4
Chalk Ridge PO8   10 E1
Chalkpit Rd PO6   23 F1
Chalkridge Rd PO6   24 C2
Chalky Walk PO16   22 B4
Chalton Cres PO9   18 D1
Chalton Ho PO1   5 G1
Chalton La PO8   8 B2
Chanctonbury Ho PO5   5 G6
Chandlers Cl PO11   33 E5
Chantry Rd PO8   10 C4
Chapel La PO7   17 G2
Chapel St, Petersfield GU32   6 C4
Chapel St, Portsmouth PO2   26 C5
Chapel St, Southsea PO5   5 F6
Chaplains Av PO8   13 F3
Chaplains Cl PO8   13 F3
Charlcot Lawn PO9   14 C5
Charles Ct PO7   17 G3
Charles Dickens St PO1   5 F3
Charles St, Petersfield GU32   6 C4
Charles St, Portsmouth PO1   5 H1
Charleston Cl PO11   32 A3
Charlesworth Dr PO7   13 F5
Charlesworth Gdns PO7   13 F5
Charlotte St PO1   5 F1
Charlton Dr GU31   6 D2
Charminster Rd PO6   13 G6
Charter Ho PO5   5 F4
Chartwell Dr PO6   20 A3
Chasewater Av PO3   27 F6
Chatburn Rd PO8   13 H4
Chatfield Av PO2   26 A4
Chatham Dr PO1   4 D6
Chatsworth Av PO6   24 C4
Chaucer Av PO6   22 D2

Chaucer Cl PO7   13 G5
Chedworth Cres PO6   23 F2
Chelmsford Rd PO2   27 E3
Chelsea Rd PO5   29 E4
Cheltenham Rd PO6   23 H3
Chepstow Ct PO7   14 B2
Cheriton Cl, Havant PO9   18 D1
Cheriton Cl, Waterlooville PO8   11 C5
Cheriton Rd PO4   30 B3
Cherry Tree Av PO8   14 B1
Cherrywood Gdns PO11   32 C3
Chervil Cl PO8   10 E3
Cheshire Way PO10   21 H4
Cheslyn Rd PO3   30 A1
Chester Pl PO5   29 E5
Chesterfield Rd PO3   27 F5
Chesterton Gdns PO8   11 A8
Chestnut Av, Havant PO9   18 B2
Chestnut Av, Southsea PO4   29 G3
Chestnut Av, Waterlooville PO8   11 D7
Chestnut Cl PO7   12 C2
Chestnut Ct PO9   15 G4
Chetwynd Rd PO4   29 F4
Chevening Ct PO4   30 A2
Chewter Cl PO4   30 A3
Chicester Av PO11   32 C5
Chichester Rd, Hayling Island PO11   35 E6
Chichester Rd, Portsmouth PO2   26 C4
Chidham Cl PO9   19 E4
Chidham Dr PO9   19 E3
Chidham Rd PO6   24 D2
Chidham Sq PO9   19 E4
Chilbolton Ct PO9   15 H6
Chilcombe Cl PO9   19 E2
Chilcote Rd PO3   27 F6
Childe Sq PO2   26 B3
Chilgrove Rd PO6   25 E3
Chilsdown Way PO7   17 G4
Chiltern Ct PO5   29 E6
Chilworth Gdns PO8   8 D4
Chipstead Rd PO6   24 B3
Chitty Rd PO4   29 H5
Chivers Cl PO5   5 G5
Christchurch Gdns PO7   25 E1
Christopher Way PO10   20 D4
Christyne Ct PO7   17 F4
Church Cl PO8   8 B2
Church La, Hambledon PO7   9 B1
Church La, Havant PO9   19 H6
Church La, North Hayling PO11   34 D4
Church Path PO8   11 F5
Church Pth PO10   20 C5
Church Rd, Hayling Island PO11   32 C3
Church Rd, Portsmouth PO1   5 H1
Church Rd, Southbourne PO10   21 H6
Church Rd, West Thorney PO10   37 F6
Church Rd, Westbourne PO10   21 E2
Church St PO1   26 C6
Church Ter PO9   15 G3
Church Vw, Emsworth PO10   21 E2
Church Vw, Southsea PO4   29 H3
Churcher Rd PO10   21 E2
Churchfield Rd GU32   7 E3
Churchill Ct, Portsmouth PO6   25 G3
Churchill Ct, Waterlooville PO8   11 C6
Churchill Dr PO10   20 C2
Churchill Sq PO4   29 H5
Churchill Yd Ind Est PO7   13 G6
Cinderford Cl PO6   23 G2
Cicular Rd PO1   5 E1
Civic Centre Rd PO9   19 E3
Clacton Rd PO6   24 A2
Claire Gdns PO8   10 E2
Clanfield Ho PO1   5 H1
Clare Gdns GU31   7 F4
Claremont Gdns PO7   17 G5
Claremont Rd PO1   29 F2

Clarence Esplande PO5   28 C5
Clarence Par PO5   28 D5
Clarence Rd PO5   29 E5
Clarence St PO1   28 D1
Clarendon Cl PO7   12 B2
Clarendon Pl PO1   29 E1
Clarendon Rd, Havant PO9   19 E5
Clarendon Rd, Portsmouth PO4,5   29 E5
Clarendon Rd, Southsea PO5   28 D5
Clarendon St PO1   29 E1
Clarkes Rd PO1   29 G1
Claxton St PO1   5 H2
Claybank Rd PO3   27 F4
Claybank Spur PO3   27 F4
Claydon Av PO4   29 H3
Cleeve Cl PO6   23 G2
Clegg Rd PO4   29 H4
Clement Attlee Way PO6   23 G3
Cleveland Rd PO5   29 F3
Cliffdale Gdns PO6   24 D2
Clifton Rd PO6   28 D5
Clifton St PO1   29 F1
Clifton Ter PO5   28 D5
Clinton Rd PO7   13 F4
Clive Gro PO16   22 B4
Clive Rd PO1   29 F1
Clock St PO1   4 C3
Clocktower Dr PO4   29 H5
Closewood Rd PO7   12 C5
Clovelly Rd, Emsworth PO10   20 C6
Clovelly Rd, Hayling Island PO11   34 D4
Clovelly Rd, Southbourne PO10   21 G5
Clovelly Rd, Southsea PO4   29 H3
Clover Ct PO7   14 A6
Cluster Ind Est PO4   29 G2
Clydebank Rd PO2   26 C5
Coachmans Halt PO7   9 B2
Coastguard Cotts PO9   34 B1
Coates Way PO7   17 G4
Cobblewood PO10   20 C3
Cobden Av PO3   27 F5
Coburg St PO1   29 E2
Cochrane Ho PO7   4 C3
Cockenden Cl PO8   8 B2
Cockleshell Gdns PO4   30 A4
Codrington Ho PO1   4 C2
Colbury Gro PO9   18 C1
Colchester Rd PO4   24 A2
Coldharbour Farm Rd PO10   11 C4
Coldhill La PO8   11 A8
Colebrook Av PO3   27 GE
Colemore Sq PO9   19 F2
Coleridge Gdns PO8   11 A7
Coleridge Rd PO6   22 D2
Colesbourne Rd PO6   23 F2
Colinton Av PO16   22 C2
College Cl PO9   9 B6
College La PO1   4 C3
College Rd, Portsmouth PO1   4 C3
College Rd, Waterlooville PO7   25 G3
College St, Petersfield GU31   6 D4
College St, Portsmouth PO1   4 C3
Collington Cres PO6   23 G3
Collingwood Rd PO5   29 E5
Collingwood Way GU31   6 D4
Collins Rd PO4   29 H5
Collis Rd PO3   27 E5
Colman Ho PO1   5 E5
Colpoy St PO5   5 F5
Coltsfoot Dr PO7   17 H5
Coltsmead PO6   23 E5
Colville Rd PO6   24 C4
Colwell Rd PO6   24 B5
Comfrey Cl PO8   10 E1
Comley Hill PO9   20 A4
Commercial Pl PO1   5 G1
Commercial Rd PO1   5 F1
Common St PO1   29 E1
Commonside PO10   21 G4
Compass Rd PO6   23 G5
Compton Cl PO9   19 C4
Compton Ct*, Chidham Cl PO9   19 E4

Compton Rd PO2 26 D2
Conan Rd PO2 26 D1
Conford Ct PO9 14 D5
Conifer Cl PO8 14 A1
Conifer Mews PO16 22 C2
Conigar Rd PO10 20 D3
Coniston Av PO3 27 E5
Connaught La PO6 22 D3
Connaught Rd, Havant PO9 19 G5
Connaught Rd, Portsmouth PO2 26 C3
Convent Ct PO10 20 C5
Convent La PO10 20 C5
Cooks La PO10 21 H5
Coombs Cl PO8 10 D3
Cooper Gro PO16 22 C5
Cooper Rd PO3 27 G5
Copnor Rd PO3 27 E1
Copper Beech Dr PO6 25 G3
Copper St PO5 5 G3
Coppins Gro PO16 22 B5
Copse Cl, Petersfield GU31 7 F3
Copse Cl, Waterlooville PO7 17 G6
Copse La PO11 35 B7
Copsey Cl PO6 25 F3
Copsey Gro PO6 25 F3
Copythorn Rd PO2 27 E4
Coral Cl PO16 22 B4
Coralin Gro PO7 14 B3
Corbett Rd PO7 17 F3
Corby Cres PO3 27 G1
Corhampton Cres PO9 18 D2
Cornaway La PO16 22 A4
Cornbrook Gro PO7 14 C2
Cornelius Dr PO7 14 B3
Corner Mead PO7 12 B3
Cornwall Rd PO1 29 F2
Cornwallis Cres PO1 29 E1
Cornwell Cl PO2 26 A3
Coronation Rd, Hayling Island PO11 33 G6
Coronation Rd, Waterlooville PO7 13 G6
Cosham Park Av PO6 24 C4
Cotswold Cl PO9 15 E6
Cottage Cl PO7 12 B3
Cottage Gro PO5 5 G5
Cottage Vw PO1 5 H2
Cotton Dr PO10 20 C2
Cotwell Av PO8 11 C8
Court Cl PO6 24 D4
Court La PO6 24 D4
Court Mead PO6 24 D3
Courtlands Ter PO8 11 C7
Courtmount Gro PO6 24 C2
Courtmount Path PO6 24 D2
Cousins Gro PO4 29 G5
Coverack Way PO6 23 G4
Covert Gro PO7 14 A6
Covington Rd PO10 21 E1
Cow La, Fareham PO16 22 C4
Cow La, Portsmouth PO5 24 A4
Cowan Rd PO7 17 G3
Cowdray Ho PO1 5 H2
Cowper Rd PO1 29 F1
Coxes Mdw GU32 6 B2
Crabbe Ct PO5 5 G4
Crabwood Ct PO9 14 D4
Craddock Ho PO1 4 C2
Crafts La GU31 6 D2
Craig Ho PO5 29 E5
Craigwell Rd PO7 17 G5
Cranborne Rd PO6 24 C2
Craneswater Av PO4 29 F6
Craneswater Gate PO4 29 F6
Craneswater Pk PO4 29 F5
Cranford Rd GU32 6 B5
Cranleigh Av PO1 29 F1
Cranleigh Rd, Fareham PO16 22 A4
Cranleigh Rd, Portsmouth PO1 29 F1
Crasswell St PO1 5 G1
Crawley Av PO9 15 G6
Crawters La GU32 6 C4
Credenhill Rd PO6 23 H2
Creech Vw PO7 12 B3
Creek End PO10 20 C6
Creek Rd PO11 33 F5
Cremorne Pl GU32 6 D4
Cressy Rd PO2 26 C6

Crestland Cl PO8 11 C8
Cricket Dr PO8 11 B6
Crinoline Gdns PO4 29 H5
Crisspyn Cl PO8 11 D6
Cristalex Ct PO8 11 B8
Crockford Rd PO10 21 E2
Croft La PO11 35 B6
Croft Rd PO2 26 C4
Crofton Cl PO7 17 F4
Crofton Rd, Portsmouth PO2 26 D3
Crofton Rd, Southsea PO4 30 A2
Cromarty Av PO4 29 H3
Crombie Cl PO8 11 B7
Cromer Rd PO6 24 A2
Cromwell Rd PO4 29 H5
Crondall Av PO9 15 E6
Crookham Cl PO9 18 C1
Crookhorn La PO7 17 H5
Cross La PO8 11 C6
Cross St, Portsmouth PO1 4 D2
Cross St, Southsea PO5 5 H4
Cross Way PO9 19 E4
Crossbill Cl PO8 11 C5
Crossland Dr PO9 19 F3
Crouch La PO8 10 B4
Crown Cl PO7 17 G5
Crown Ct PO1 4 D5
Crown St PO1 29 E1
Crowsbury Cl PO10 20 C2
Croxton Rd PO1 5 E6
Crundles GU32 7 E4
Crystal Way PO7 14 A4
Culver Dr PO11 33 E6
Culver Rd PO4 29 H5
Culverin Sq PO3 24 C6

Cumberland Bsns Centre PO5 29 E2
Cumberland Ho PO1 4 D1
Cumberland St PO1 4 D1
Cunningham Cl PO2 24 A6
Cunningham Rd, Horndean PO8 11 D5
Cunningham Rd, Waterlooville PO7 17 G3
Curdridge Cl PO9 19 G1
Curie Rd PO6 24 B2
Curlew Cl PO10 20 C6
Curlew Gdns PO8 11 A7
Curtis Mead PO2 27 E1
Curzon Howe Rd PO1 4 D2
Curzon Rd PO7 17 G1
Cuthbert Rd PO1 29 G1
Cygnet Rd PO6 25 H3
Cypress Cres PO8 11 B7
Cyprus Rd PO2 26 C6

Daisy Mead PO7 14 A5
Dale Ho PO1 5 H2
Damask Gdns PO7 14 A5
Danbury Ct PO10 20 D3
Dances Way PO11 32 A3
Dando Rd PO7 12 C3
Danebury Cl PO9 15 E5
Danes Rd PO16 22 A1
Danesbrook La PO7 14 A5
Darby Ho PO1 24 C2
Dark Hollow GU32 6 B3
Darlington Rd PO4 29 F4
Dartmouth Mews PO5 5 E6
Dartmouth Rd PO3 27 E3
Darwin Ho PO1 5 H2
Daubeney Gdns PO9 14 C6
Daulston Rd PO1 26 D6
Daventry La PO3 25 E6
Davidia Ct PO7 14 A6
Davidson Cl PO7 4 D3
Daw La PO11 35 A7
Day La PO8 11 A5
Dayslondon Rd PO7 17 F3
De Lisle Cl PO7 27 E1
Deal Rd PO6 24 A2
Dean Rd PO6 24 C3
Dean St PO1 4 D3
Deane Ct PO9 19 H1
Deanswood Dr PO7 13 G5
Deep Dell PO8 11 D7
Deeping Gate PO7 14 A4
Deerhurst Cres PO6 23 F2
Delamere Rd PO4 29 F4
Delaval Ho PO1 5 H2
Delft Gdns PO8 13 G4
Delius Walk PO7 17 G4
Dell Cl PO7 24 D1
Dell Cotts PO10 21 H1
Dell Piece East PO8 11 E6

Dell Piece West PO8 11 D6
Dellcrest Path PO7 24 D1
Dellfield Cl PO6 23 F2
Delphi Way PO7 17 H6
Dene Hollow PO6 25 H1
Denhill Cl PO11 32 A2
Denmead Ho PO1 5 H1
Denmead Pk PO7 12 D3
Denning Mews PO5 5 G3
Denville Av PO16 22 C5
Denville Cl PO6 25 H3
Derby Rd PO2 26 C4
Dersingham Cl PO6 24 D3
Derwent Cl PO8 10 E1
Desborough Cl PO6 23 F2
Deverell Pl PO7 17 E6
Devon Rd PO3 27 F2
Devonshire Av PO4 29 G3
Devonshire Sq PO4 29 G3
Diamond Ct PO7 13 G6
Diamond St PO5 5 H4
Diana Cl PO10 20 C2
Dibden Ct PO9 18 C1
Dickens Cl PO2 26 C6
Dickens Ho PO4 30 A3
Dickins La GU31 6 D2
Dickinson Rd PO4 29 G2
Dieppe Cres PO2 26 C1
Ditcham Cres PO9 19 E2
Dobson Cl PO8 11 A7
Dockenfield Cl PO9 18 B2
Dogwood Dell PO7 17 H3
Dolphin Ct PO4 29 F6
Domum Rd PO2 27 E3
Domvilles App PO2 26 A4
Donaldson Rd PO6 24 B5
Dorcas St PO5 5 F4
Dore Av PO16 22 A3
Dorking Cres PO6 24 C4
Dormington Rd PO6 23 G2
Dornmere La PO7 14 A4
Dorothy Dymond St PO1 5 F3
Dorrita Av PO8 11 B8
Dorrita Cl PO4 29 F5
Dorset Cl PO8 11 D5
Dorstone Rd PO6 23 H2
Douglas Gdns PO9 19 G1
Douglas Rd PO3 27 E6
Dover Ct PO11 32 B2
Dover Rd PO3 27 F5
Dovercourt Rd PO6 24 D5
Dowell Ho*, Gunners Row PO4 30 A5
Down End Rd PO6 25 E2
Down End PO6 25 E2
Down Farm Pl PO8 10 E3
Down Rd PO8 10 D2
Downham Cl PO8 13 H4
Downhouse Rd PO8 8 B4
Downley Rd PO9 19 H2
Downs Cl PO7 17 H5
Downside Rd PO7 17 E6
Downwood Way PO8 10 D2
Doyle Av PO3 26 D1
Doyle Cl PO2 26 D1

Dragon Est PO6 25 G4
Dragon St GU32 6 C5
Drake Ho PO1 4 C2
Draycote Rd PO8 10 E1
Drayton La PO6 25 E2
Drayton Rd PO2 26 D4
Dresden Dr PO8 13 G4
Drift Rd PO8 8 A3
Driftwood Gdns PO4 30 B5
Drum Cl GU32 6 C4
Drum La GU32 6 C4
Drum Mead GU32 6 C4
Drummond Rd PO1 5 H1
Dryden Av PO6 22 D2
Dryden Ct PO7 13 G5
Drysdale Mews PO4 30 A5
Duckworth Ho PO1 4 D3
Dudledon Heath Dr PO8 14 B1
Dudley Rd PO8 27 E6
Duffield La PO10 21 G2
Dugald Drummond St PO1 5 G3
Duisburg Way PO5 28 C4
Duke Cres PO6 26 C6
Duke of Edinburgh Ho PO1 4 D1
Dukes Cl, Emsworth PO10 21 E2
Dukes Cl, Petersfield GU32 6 A3
Dukes Walk PO7 17 G2

Dukes Walk Service Rd PO7 17 G2
Dumbarton Cl PO2 26 C5
Dummer Ct PO8 10 A3
Dunbar Rd PO4 30 A5
Duncan Cooper Ho PO7 17 F2
Duncan Rd PO5 29 E5
Duncton Rd PO8 8 D3
Dundas Cl PO3 27 F3
Dundas La PO3 27 G4
Dundas Spur PO3 27 F3
Dundonald Cl PO11 32 C2
Dunhurst Cl PO9 19 G2
Dunlin Cl PO4 30 B2
Dunn Cl PO4 30 A4
Dunnock Cl PO9 9 B6
Dunsbury Way PO16 15 E6
Dunsmore Cl PO5 5 G4
Dupree Dr PO4 29 H4
Durban Rd PO1 27 E6
Durford Ct PO9 14 D5
Durford Rd GU31 7 F4
Durham Gdns PO7 17 H4
Durham St PO1 5 G2
Durlands Rd PO8 10 D4
Durley Av PO8 11 A8
Durrants Gdns PO9 15 G4
Durrants Rd PO9 15 G4
Dursley Cres PO6 23 H3
Dymoke St PO10 20 B3
Dymond Ho PO4 30 A3
Dysart Av PO6 24 D4

Eagle Av PO8 13 G3
Earlsdon St PO5 5 F4
Earnley Rd PO11 33 G5
East Cosham Rd PO6 24 D3
East Ct, Cosham PO6 24 D3
East Ct, Kingston PO1 26 D6
East Field Cl PO10 21 H4
East Lodge Pk PO6 25 H3
East Meon Rd PO8 8 A1
East St, Fareham PO16 22 C3
East St, Havant PO9 19 F5
East St, Portsmouth PO1 4 B5
East St, Waterlooville PO7 9 C2
East Surrey St PO1 5 G2
Eastbourne Rd PO3 27 F5
Eastern Av PO3 30 A1
Eastern Ind Centre PO6 25 F4
Eastern Par PO4 29 G6
Eastern Rd, Drayton PO3 25 F5
Eastern Rd, Havant PO9 19 F4
Eastern Rd, Portsea Island PO3 27 H1
Eastern Rd, Portsmouth PO3 30 A2
Eastern Rd, Whale Island PO2 26 A3
Eastfield Rd, Fareham PO17 23 G1
Eastfield Rd, Southsea PO4 29 H4
Eastlake Cl GU31 7 F4
Eastlake Heights PO4 30 C4
Eastleigh Rd PO9 30 A2
Eastney Esp PO4 29 H6
Eastney Farm Rd PO4 30 A4
Eastney Rd PO4 30 A4
Eastney St PO4 29 H5
Eastoke Av PO11 33 F6
Eastover Ct PO9 14 D5
Eastwood Cl PO11 32 D2
Eastwood Rd PO2 26 D1
Ebery Gro PO3 27 G6
Ecton La PO3 27 G1
Eden St PO1 5 G1
Edenbridge Rd PO4 30 A2
Edgar Cres PO16 22 C4
Edgbaston Ho PO5 5 G4
Edgefield Gro PO7 14 C3
Edgell Rd PO10 21 E2
Edgerly Gdns PO6 24 C5
Edgeware Rd PO4 29 H2
Edinburgh Ho PO6 24 B3
Edinburgh Rd PO1 5 E2
Edmund Rd PO4 29 F4
Edneys La PO7 12 D1
Edward Gdns PO9 18 C4
Edward Gro PO16 22 D2
Edwards Cl, Portsmouth PO6 23 G2

Edwards Cl, Waterlooville PO8 13 H5
Egan Cl PO2 27 E1
Eglantine Cl PO8 11 D8
Eglantine Walk PO8 11 D8
Elaine Gdns PO8 11 B6
Elder Rd PO9 19 H3
Elderberry Cl PO8 8 D4
Elderberry Way PO8 11 D7
Elderfield Cl PO10 20 D3
Elderfield Rd PO9 14 D4
Eldon Ct PO5 5 F4
Eldon St PO5 5 F5
Eleanors Wood PO16 22 A2
Elettra Av PO7 13 F6
Elgar Cl PO6 22 D3
Elgar Walk PO7 17 H4
Elgin Rd PO6 24 C5
Eling Ct PO9 14 D5
Elizabeth Gdns PO4 29 G5
Elizabeth Rd PO7 17 G4
Elkstone Rd PO6 23 G2
Ellesmere Orch PO10 21 E1
Ellisfield Rd PO9 19 E1
Elm Close Est PO11 32 B4
Elm Gro, Hayling Island PO11 32 C3
Elm Gro, Southsea PO5 5 G5
Elm La PO9 19 E4
Elm Park Rd PO9 19 F4
Elm Rd PO9 19 G5
Elm St PO5 5 F6
Elmeswelle Rd PO8 11 B6
Elmleigh Rd PO9 19 E3
Elmtree Rd PO6 25 G2
Elmwood Av PO7 17 G2
Elmwood Rd PO2 26 D1
Elphinstone Rd PO5 28 D5
Elsie Fudge Ho PO7 17 H6
Elstead Gdns PO7 17 E5
Elwell Grn PO11 32 B4
Emanuel St PO2 26 C6
Emerald Cl PO7 14 A4
Empshott Rd PO4 29 G3
Emsbrook Dr PO10 20 D4
Emsworth Common Rd PO9 20 B1
Emsworth House Cl PO10 20 B5
Emsworth Rd, Emsworth PO10 36 C3
Emsworth Rd, Havant PO9 19 G5
Emsworth Rd, Portsmouth PO2 26 D4
Endeavour Bsns Pk PO9 19 E6
Enderleigh Ho PO9 18 D4
Ennerdale Cl PO10 20 E2
Enterprise Centre PO3 27 G2
Enterprise Ind Est PO8 10 E4
Enterprise Rd PO8 11 B5
Eperston Rd PO8 11 B5
Epworth Rd PO2 27 E4
Eric Ct PO4 29 F4
Erica Cl PO8 11 D8
Erica Way PO8 11 D8
Ernest Ct PO10 20 C5
Ernest Rd, Havant PO9 18 C2
Ernest Rd, Portsmouth PO1 26 D6
Escur Ct PO2 27 E1
Esher Gro PO7 13 G5
Eskdale Cl PO8 10 D2
Esmond Cl PO10 20 C6
Esplanade Gdns PO4 30 A5
Essex Rd PO4 29 H3
Esslemont Rd PO4 29 F4
Estella Rd PO2 26 B5
Ethel Rd PO1 29 F1
Eton Rd PO5 29 F1
Euston Rd PO4 29 H2
Eva Allaway Ct PO1 4 D3
Evans Cl PO2 26 A3
Evans Rd PO4 29 H3
Everdon La PO3 27 G1
Everglades Av PO8 11 D8
Evergreen Cl PO7 17 F2
Eversley Cres PO9 18 D1
Ewart Rd PO1 26 D6
Ewhurst Cl PO9 18 D1
Exbury Rd PO9 15 G6
Exchange Rd PO1 5 F3
Exeter Cl PO10 20 C3
Exeter Rd PO4 29 G5

xmouth Rd PO5 29 E5
xton Gdns PO16 22 B1
xton Rd PO9 19 H1
Faber Cl PO9 19 G1
Fabian Cl PO7 14 A3
Fair Oak Dr PO9 19 F3
Fair Oak Rd PO4 30 B3
Fairbourne Cl PO8 13 G4
Fairfield Cl PO10 20 C3
Fairfield Rd PO9 19 F4
Fairfield Sq PO6 24 A2
Fairlea Rd PO10 20 D3
Fairley Ct GU31 6 D4
Fairmead Ct PO11 32 A4
Fairmead Walk PO8 11 C8
Fairway Bsns Centre PO3 27 G2
Fairy Cross Way PO8 14 B1
Falcon Grn PO6 25 H4
Falcon Rd PO8 11 C5
Falkland Rd PO2 26 C1
Falmouth Rd PO6 23 E2
Far Meadow Way PO10 20 B5
Farleigh Cl PO9 14 D6
Farlington Av PO6 25 E2
Farlington Rd PO2 26 D4
Farm Lane Cl PO7 17 G3
Farm View Av PO8 8 C3
Farm Vw PO10 20 C2
Farmhouse Way PO8 11 B7
Farmlea Rd PO6 23 E3
Farmside Gdns PO3 24 C6
Farnham Rd GU32 7 E1
Farriers Way PO7 14 C2
Farringdon Rd PO9 19 G2
Farthing La PO1 4 D6
Farthings Gate PO7 17 G6
Fastnet Ho PO5 29 E6
Fathoms Reach PO11 32 B3
Fawcett Rd PO4 29 F4
Fawley Cl PO9 19 H1
Fawley Rd PO2 24 B6
Fearon Rd PO2 26 D3
Feltons Pl PO3 24 C6
Fennell Cl PO7 13 F6
Fern Cl GU31 7 F5
Fern Dr PO9 19 G3
Ferndale PO7 17 H1
Fernhurst Cl PO11 32 A4
Fernhurst Rd PO4 29 G3
Ferry Rd, Eastney PO4 30 B4
Ferry Rd, Hayling Island PO11 31 E3
Ferry Rd, Langstone Harbour PO4 29 G5
Festing Gro PO4 29 G5
Festing Rd PO4 29 G5
Festival Ct*, Heath Rd GU31 6 D4
Field Way PO7 12 C3
Fielders Ct PO7 17 F4
Fieldfare Cl PO8 8 C4
Fifth Av, Havant PO9 19 H3
Fifth Av, Portsmouth PO6 24 B3
Fifth St PO1 27 E6
Finch Ho PO4 30 A5
Finch Rd PO4 30 B4
Finchdean Rd, Havant PO9 18 D1
Finchdean Rd, Rowlands Castle PO9 9 C5
Finchwood Fm Ind Units PO11 35 C6
Fir Copse Rd PO7 17 F5
Fir Tree Gdns PO8 11 D7
Fir Tree Rd PO11 32 C4
Firgrove Cres PO3 24 B6
Firlands Rise PO9 18 A5
Firs Av PO8 13 H5
Firs Pk GU31 7 F4
First Av, Cosham PO6 24 B3
First Av, Emsworth PO10 21 G5
First Av, Farlington PO6 25 G3
First Av, Havant PO9 19 G4
First Av, Waterlooville PO8 10 E1
Fishermans Walk, Fareham PO16 22 C4
Fishermans Walk, Hayling Island PO11 33 G5
Fishers Gro PO6 25 G4
Fishery La PO11 33 E5
Fitzherbert Rd PO6 25 F4
Fitzherbert Spur PO6 25 G3

Fitzherbert St PO1 26 B6
Fitzpatrick Ct PO6 23 H2
Fitzroy Walk PO1 29 E1
Fitzwygram Cres PO9 19 F3
Five Heads Rd PO8 10 C3
Five Walk PO8 11 B7
Flathouse Rd PO1 26 B5
Fleet End Cl PO9 15 E5
Flexford Gdns PO9 19 G2
Flinders Ct PO4 30 A5
Flint St PO5 5 E6
Florence Rd PO4 29 E6
Florentine Way PO7 14 B3
Flying Bull Cl PO2 26 C5
Folkestone Rd PO3 27 F5
Folly La GU31 6 C4
Fontwell Mews PO7 14 B2
Fontwell Rd PO5 29 E5
Forbes Ct PO2 26 D2
Forbury Rd PO5 5 H3
Fordingbridge Rd PO4 30 A4
Fore Bri GU32 6 C5
Foreland Ct PO11 33 E5
Forest Av PO8 11 B8
Forest Cl PO8 11 B8
Forest End PO7 17 F2
Forest Mead PO7 12 C3
Forest Rd, Denmead PO7 12 A2
Forest Rd, Waterlooville PO7 17 F2
Forestside Av PO9 15 G6
Forsythia Cl PO9 19 H2
Fort Cumberland Rd PO4 30 B4
Forton Rd PO1 29 F1
Fortunes Way PO9 25 H2
Foster Rd PO1 29 E1
Foundry Ct PO1 4 D2
Fountain Sq PO11 32 A3
Fountain St PO1 5 F2
Fourth Av, Havant PO9 19 G4
Fourth Av, Portsmouth PO6 24 B3
Fourth St PO1 29 G1
Foxbury Gro PO16 22 A4
Foxbury La PO10 21 E2
Foxcott Gro PO9 19 E1
Foxes Cl PO7 17 G2
Foxley Dr PO3 27 G1
Frances Rd PO7 17 F5
Francis Av PO4 29 F5
Francis Rd PO8 10 E1
Frank Judd Ct PO1 4 D3
Frank Miles Ho PO5 5 G5
Frankland Ter PO10 20 D5
Frarydene PO7 21 G6
Fraser Gdns PO10 21 H4
Fraser Rd, Havant PO9 18 D3
Fraser Rd, Portsmouth PO2 26 D3
Fraser Rd, Southsea PO5 5 H4
Fratton Ind Est PO4 29 G2
Fratton Rd PO1 26 D6
Fratton Way PO4 29 G3
Frederick St PO1 28 D1
Freestone Rd PO5 29 E5
French St PO1 4 C5
Frenchies Vw PO7 12 B2
Frenchmans Rd GU32 6 B4
Frendstaple Rd PO7 14 A5
Frensham Rd PO4 29 G3
Freshfield Gdns PO7 17 G1
Freshwater Rd PO6 24 B6
Friary Cl PO7 29 E5
Frobisher Gdns*, School La PO10 20 D6
Frobisher Gro PO16 22 B4
Frobisher Ho PO1 4 C2
Froddington Rd PO5 29 E2
Frogham Grn PO9 14 C5
Frogmore La PO8 11 B7
Frogmore Rd PO4 29 G3
Froxfield Gdns PO16 22 B2
Froxfield Rd PO9 15 H6
Froyle Ct PO9 19 H1
Fulflood Rd PO9 15 E6
Fullerton Ct PO9 15 H6
Fulmer Walk PO8 11 A8
Funtington Rd PO2 27 E5
Furdies PO7 12 B3
Furlonge Ho PO10 20 B5
Furness Rd PO5 29 E5
Furniss Way PO11 32 A3
Furnston Gro PO10 21 H5

Furze La PO4 30 B2
Furze Way PO8 11 D7
Furzedown Cres PO9 15 G6
Furzeley Rd PO7 12 B5
Furzley Ct PO9 14 D6
Fushia Cl PO9 19 H2
Fyning St PO1 5 H1
Gable Mews PO11 32 C3
Gains Rd PO4 29 F5
Galaxie Rd PO8 11 C8
Galt Rd PO6 25 G2
Gamble Rd PO2 26 C5
Gammon Cl GU31 6 D3
Garden Cl PO11 32 B4
Garden Ct PO16 22 C3
Garden La PO5 5 F6
Garden Mews GU32 6 C4
Garden Ter PO9 29 E5
Garfield Rd PO2 26 C5
Garland Av PO10 20 C3
Garnier St PO1 29 E2
Garsons Rd PO10 21 G6
Gatcombe Av PO3 27 E2
Gatcombe Dr PO2 26 D1
Gaulter Cl PO9 19 G3
Geddes Way GU31 7 F3
Genoa Ho PO6 23 F4
Geoffrey Av PO7 16 D6
George Byng Way PO2 26 B5
George Cotts PO7 9 C2
George Ho PO7 9 C2
George St PO1 26 D6
Gibraltar Rd PO4 30 B4
Gilbert Mead PO11 32 A3
Gilbert Way PO7 17 G3
Gillman Rd PO6 25 G2
Gisors Rd PO4 30 A3
Gitsham Gdns PO7 17 F6
Gladstone Gdns PO16 22 B4
Gladstone Pl PO2 26 C5
Gladys Av, Waterlooville PO8 11 B8
Gladys Av, Portsmouth PO2 26 C2
Glamis Cl PO7 14 A4
Glamorgan Rd PO8 10 D2
Glasgow Rd PO4 30 A4
Glasspool PO7 12 A2
Glebe Cl PO11 32 A2
Glebe Ho PO10 21 G6
Glebe Park Av PO3 18 A4
Glebefield Gdns PO6 24 A3
Glencoe Rd PO1 26 D6
Glendale PO9 9 C6
Gleneagles Dr PO7 14 B2
Glenleigh Av PO6 24 C3
Glenleigh Pk PO9 19 H4
Glenthorne Rd PO3 27 F4
Glenwood Gdns PO8 13 H4
Glenwood Rd PO10 21 H4
Glidden Cl PO1 5 H2
Glidden La PO7 9 D1
Gloucester Cl GU32 6 B4
Gloucester Mews PO5 5 F5
Gloucester Pl PO5 5 F5
Gloucester Rd, Portsmouth PO1 4 C1
Gloucester Rd, Waterlooville PO7 17 H3
Gloucester Ter PO5 5 F5
Gloucester Vw PO5 5 F5
Godiva Lawn PO4 30 B4
Godwin Cl PO10 20 C2
Godwin Cres PO8 8 C4
Godwit Rd PO4 30 B1
Gofton Av PO6 24 D4
Gold St PO5 5 E6
Goldcrest Cl PO8 11 C5
Golden Ct PO7 17 G1
Goldring Cl PO11 32 D4
Goldsmith Av PO4 29 F2
Goodwood Cl PO8 14 B2
Goodwood Ct PO10 21 H6
Goodwood Rd PO5 29 F4
Gordon Rd, Emsworth PO10 21 E6
Gordon Rd, Portsmouth PO1 5 E6
Gordon Rd, Waterlooville PO7 17 F3
Goring Av PO8 8 D4
Gorley Ct PO9 19 H1
Gorse Rd GU31 7 F5
Gorseway PO11 34 H4
Grafton St PO2 26 B6
Graham Rd PO4 29 F4
Granada Cl PO8 11 C8

Granada Rd PO4 29 E6
Grand Par, Hayling Island PO11 32 C5
Grand Par, Portsmouth PO1 4 C6
Granden Ct PO9 19 E4
Grange Cl PO9 19 G4
Grange Rd, Petersfield GU32 6 B5
Grange Rd, Portsmouth PO2 26 C4
Grant Rd PO5 25 G2
Granville Cl PO9 19 G5
Grassmere Way PO7 14 B2
Grateley Cres PO9 18 C1
Grayland Cl PO11 32 A3
Grays Ct PO1 4 D4
Grayshott Rd PO4 29 G3
Great Copse Dr PO9 15 E6
Great Hanger GU32 7 E4
Great Mead PO7 12 D4
Greatfield Way PO9 9 B5
Grebe Cl, Emsworth PO10 21 F2
Grebe Cl, Waterlooville PO8 11 A8
Green Farm Gdns PO3 27 E1
Green La, Clanfield PO8 8 A1
Green La, Clanfield PO8 8 D4
Green La, Denmead PO7 12 B2
Green La, Hambledon PO7 9 A1
Green La, Hayling Island PO11 32 A5
Green La, Portsmouth PO3 27 E2
Green Mdws PO7 12 B2
Green Rd PO5 5 F5
Greenacre Gdns PO7 17 F5
Greenfield Cres PO8 11 D7
Greenfield Rise PO8 11 D8
Greenlea Ct PO7 24 D1
Greenwood Av PO6 24 A3
Greetham St PO1 5 G3
Grenhurst Way GU31 6 D4
Grenfield Cl PO10 20 C2
Grenville Ho PO1 4 D3
Grenville Rd PO4 29 F4
Greville Grn PO10 20 C2
Greyfriars Ct PO5 5 G6
Greywell Rd PO9 19 E1
Grindle Cl PO16 22 B2
Gritanwood Rd PO4 30 A4
Grosvenor Ho PO5 5 G4
Grosvenor St PO5 5 G4
Grove Av PO16 22 B5
Grove Ct PO9 19 F5
Grove Ho, Cottage Gro PO5 5 H5
Grove Ho, Hendy Cl PO5 5 G6
Grove Rd, Havant PO9 19 F5
Grove Rd, Portsmouth PO6 25 E4
Grove Rd North PO5 5 G6
Grove Rd South PO5 5 G6
Gruneisen Rd PO2 26 B3
Guardhouse Rd PO1 26 A6
Guardroom Rd PO2 26 A4
Guildford Cl PO10 21 H5
Guildford Rd PO1 29 F1
Guildhall Sq PO1 5 F3
Guildhall Walk PO1 5 F3
Gunners Row PO4 30 A5
Gunstore Rd PO3 27 F1
Gunwharf Quays Retail & Leisure Pk PO1 4 C3
Gunwharf Rd PO1 4 C5
Gurnard Rd PO6 24 B6
Gurney Rd PO4 30 A3
Gutner La PO11 35 D6
Gwatkin Cl PO11 18 B3
Gypsy La PO8 11 B6
Hadleigh Rd PO6 24 A2
Haig Ct PO2 26 D6
Hale Ct PO1 26 D6
Hale St North PO1 29 E1
Hale St South PO1 29 E1
Halesowen Ho PO5 5 F4
Half Moon St PO1 4 C2
Halfpenny La PO1 4 D3
Halfpenny La PO7 17 H2
Halifax Rise PO7 17 H2
Hallett Rd PO9 19 H4
Halliday Cres PO4 30 B4

Halliday Ho*, Gunners Row PO4 30 A5
Halstead Rd PO6 24 A3
Ham La, Emsworth PO10 21 G6
Ham La, Waterlooville PO8 10 B4
Hamble La PO7 17 G3
Hambledon Par PO7 13 E5
Hambledon Rd, Clanfield PO8 8 A2
Hambledon Rd, Denmead PO7 12 A1
Hambrook St PO5 5 E6
Hamfield Dr PO11 32 A3
Hamilton Cl PO9 19 F6
Hamilton Rd, Portsmouth PO6 22 D3
Hamilton Rd, Southsea PO5 29 E5
Hampage Grn PO9 14 D5
Hampshire St PO1 26 D6
Hampshire Ter PO1 5 E4
Hampton Cl PO7 14 A4
Hanbury Sq GU31 6 D2
Handsworth Ho PO5 5 H3
Hanger Way GU32 7 E4
Hannah Gdns PO7 13 H6
Hannington Rd PO9 14 D5
Hanover Ct PO1 4 D5
Hanover St PO1 4 C2
Hanway Rd PO2 26 C5
Ha'penny Dell PO7 17 G6
Harbour Ct PO10 20 D6
Harbour Rd PO11 31 G3
Harbour Vw PO16 22 B5
Harbour Way, Emsworth PO10 20 D6
Harbour Way, Portsmouth PO2 26 B5
Harbourside PO9 34 A1
Harbridge Ct PO9 14 D5
Harcourt Cl PO8 11 B7
Harcourt Rd PO1 26 D6
Hardy Av GU31 6 D2
Harestock Rd PO9 18 D3
Harkness Dr PO7 14 B3
Harleston Rd PO4 24 A2
Harley Walk PO1 29 E1
Harold Rd, Emsworth PO10 21 E2
Harold Rd, Hayling Island PO11 32 D5
Harold Rd, Southsea PO4 29 F4
Harold Ter PO10 20 C5
Harrier Cl PO8 11 C5
Harrier Way GU31 7 F5
Harrow La GU32 6 C2
Harrow Rd PO5 29 F3
Hart Plain Av PO8 13 G3
Hartford Ho PO1 5 E5
Harting Cl PO8 8 D4
Harting Down GU32 7 E4
Harting Gdns PO16 22 B2
Hartland Ct PO10 21 G5
Hartley Rd PO2 26 C2
Harts Farm Cotts PO9 18 D5
Harts Farm Way PO9 18 B6
Hartwell Rd PO3 27 G1
Hartwood Gdns PO8 13 H4
Harvest Rd PO2 12 A2
Harvestgate Walk PO9 14 D6
Harvey Rd PO6 24 B2
Harwich Rd PO4 24 A2
Haslar Cres PO7 13 E5
Haslemere Gdns PO11 33 G5
Haslemere Rd, Emsworth PO10 21 G4
Haslemere Rd, Southsea PO4 29 G5
Hastings Ho PO2 26 B3
Hatch Ct PO9 14 C5
Hatfield Rd PO4 29 H4
Hathaway Gdns PO7 14 B3
Hatherley Cres PO16 22 A4
Hatherley Dr PO16 22 A3
Hatherley Rd PO2 23 F2
Havant Bsns Centre PO9 18 D6
Havant By-Pass PO9 18 C5
Havant Farm Cl PO9 19 F3
Havant Rd, Cosham PO6 24 C3
Havant Rd, Emsworth PO9 19 H5
Havant Rd, Hayling Island PO11 33 B4

41

Havant Rd, Stamshaw PO2 26 C4
Havant Rd, Waterlooville PO8 11 F5
Havant St PO1 4 C2
Havelock Rd PO5 29 E3
Haven Rd PO11 33 F6
Havisham Rd PO2 26 B5
Hawke St PO1 4 C2
Hawkewood Av PO7 13 F4
Hawkley Cl PO9 15 E5
Hawthorn Cl PO16 22 A2
Hawthorn Cres PO6 24 C4
Hawthorn Ct GU31 7 F5
Hawthorn Rd, Catherington PO8 10 E2
Hawthorn Rd, Denmead PO7 12 A2
Hawthorne Gro PO11 32 C3
Hayes Ct PO5 5 H5
Hayling Av PO8 27 F6
Hayward Bsns Centre PO9 19 G2
Haywards Ct PO9 4 C5
Hazel Gro PO8 8 C3
Hazel Rd PO8 8 D3
Hazelbank Cl GU32 7 E3
Hazeldean Ct PO9 15 G3
Hazeley Grn PO9 19 H1
Hazelholt Dr PO9 15 E5
Hazelwood Av PO9 18 B3
Hazleton Way PO8 11 D6
Head Down GU32 7 E4
Heath Rd PO8 11 C5
Heath Rd GU31 6 D4
Heath Rd East GU32 7 E6
Heath Rd West GU31 6 D5
Heathcote Rd PO2 27 E3
Heather Cl PO7 17 H2
Heather Rd GU31 7 F5
Heatherton Mews PO10 20 C3
Heathfield, Petersfield GU31 7 F4
Heathfield, Portsmouth PO2 26 C4
Heckfield Cl PO9 15 H6
Hector Cl PO7 17 H6
Hedge End Walk PO9 15 H6
Hedgerow Gdns PO10 20 C2
Heidelberg Rd PO4 29 G5
Helena Rd PO4 29 G5
Hellyer Rd PO4 29 H4
Helston Dr PO10 20 C3
Helston Rd PO6 23 E2
Hemlock Rd PO8 13 G3
Hempsted Rd PO6 23 E2
Hemsley Walk PO8 11 B8
Henderson Rd PO4 30 A4
Hendy Cl PO5 5 H6
Henley Rd PO4 29 G4
Henwood Down GU32 7 E4
Herbert Rd PO4 29 F5
Herbert St PO1 26 B6
Hercules St PO2 26 C6
Hereford Rd PO5 5 H6
Hermitage Cl PO9 19 E2
Hermitage Gdns PO7 17 H1
Herne Cl GU31 6 D5
Herne Rd, Petersfield GU31 6 D4
Herne Rd, Portsmouth PO6 24 A3
Heron Cl PO4 30 A2
Heron Quay PO10 36 C1
Herons Ct PO11 32 D2
Herriot Ho PO18 14 A1
Herriott Cl PO8 11 B7
Hertford Pl PO1 26 C6
Herwood Rd PO4 30 A3
Hewett Rd PO2 26 D3
Heyshott Gdns PO8 8 D4
Heyshott Rd PO4 29 F3
Heyward Rd PO4 29 F3
Heywood Gdns PO9 14 D5
High Lawn Way PO9 19 E1
High St, Cosham PO6 24 B4
High St, Emsworth PO10 20 D5
High St, Petersfield GU32 6 C4
High St, Portsmouth PO1 4 C6
High St, Waterlooville PO7 9 C2
High Trees PO7 13 H6
High Vw PO16 22 B1
ighbank Av PO8 17 E6

Highbury Gro PO6 24 C5
Highbury St PO1 4 D5
Highbury Way PO6 24 B5
Highclere Av PO9 18 D1
Highcroft Ind Est PO8 10 E4
Highcroft La PO8 10 E4
Highfield Av PO7 13 H6
Highfield Cl PO7 13 H6
Highfield Par PO7 14 A3
Highfield Rd, Petersfield GU32 6 C3
Highfield Rd, Portsmouth PO1 5 H2
Highgate Rd PO3 27 F4
Highgrove Ind Pk PO3 27 G2
Highgrove Lodge PO6 25 E4
Highgrove Rd PO3 27 F5
Highland Cl PO10 20 C5
Highland Rd, Emsworth PO10 20 C5
Highland Rd, Southsea PO4 29 G5
Highland St PO4 29 H5
Highland Ter PO4 29 G4
Highlands Rd PO6 25 F2
Highwood Lawn PO9 14 D5
Higworth La PO11 32 B2
Hilary Av PO6 24 C4
Hilda Gdns PO7 12 C3
Hilden Ct PO11 32 B4
Hill Brow Cl PO9 9 B6
Hill Rd PO16 22 C1
Hill View Rd PO16 22 B2
Hillborough Cres PO9 29 E4
Hilldowns Av PO2 26 B2
Hillmead Gdns PO8 18 B3
Hillside Av PO7 24 D1
Hillside Cl PO8 10 E1
Hillside Cres PO6 23 E2
Hillside Ind Est PO8 10 E3
Hillsley Rd PO6 22 D1
Hilltop Cres PO6 25 E1
Hilltop Gdns PO8 10 E1
Hillview PO8 11 E6
Hilsea Cres PO2 26 A6
Hilsea Lodge PO2 26 D2
Hiltingbury Rd PO9 15 G6
Hinton Cl PO9 18 C1
Hinton Daubnay Rd PO8 10 B1
Hinton Manor Barns PO8 10 B1
Hinton Manor La, Catherington PO8 10 A3
Hinton Manor La, Clanfield PO8 8 A4
Hipley Rd PO9 19 F3
Hither Grn PO10 21 H4
Hitherwood Cl PO7 14 B3
Hoadlands GU32 7 E4
Hobbs Sq GU31 6 D3
Hobby Cl, Portsmouth PO3 27 E1
Hobby Cl, Waterlooville PO8 11 A7
Hockham Ct PO9 14 A7
Hockley Cl PO6 24 A3
Hodges Cl PO9 19 G3
Hoggarth Cl GU31 6 D3
Holbeach Cl PO6 24 A2
Holbrook Rd PO1 5 H1
Holbury Ct PO9 15 G6
Holcot La PO3 27 G1
Holdenhurst Cl PO8 10 E3
Hollam Rd PO4 30 A2
Holland Rd PO4 29 F3
Hollow La PO11 32 B4
Holly Dr PO7 14 A5
Hollybank Cl PO8 11 E7
Hollybank La PO10 20 C1
Hollywell Dr PO8 23 F4
Holm Ct PO11 32 B5
Holman Cl PO8 8 D2
Holmbush Ct PO5 5 G6
Holne Ct PO4 30 B4
Holst Way PO8 17 H4
Holt Down GU32 7 E4
Holt Gdns PO9 9 B4
Holybourne Rd PO9 19 E3
Holyrood Ct PO7 14 A4
Home Mead PO7 12 B3
Home Way GU31 7 F4
Homefield Path PO8 25 E4
Homefield Rd, Emsworth PO10 21 E2

Homefield Rd, Portsmouth PO6 25 E4
Homefield Way PO8 8 B2
Homegrove Ho PO5 5 H5
Homer Ct PO8 13 G4
Homerose Ho PO5 5 G5
Homesea Ho PO5 5 G5
Homestead Ct PO8 8 D1
Homewater Ho PO7 17 H1
Homewell PO9 19 F5
Honeysuckle Ct PO7 14 A6
Honeywood Ct PO3 27 E1
Hooks Farm Way PO9 18 D3
Hooks La PO9 18 C3
Hopfield Cl PO7 17 G2
Hopfield Mews PO7 17 G2
Hopkins Cl PO6 22 D3
Hopkins Ct PO4 30 A5
Hordle La PO9 18 B1
Hornbeam Rd PO9 19 H3
Horndean Ho PO1 5 H1
Horndean Rd PO10 20 A1
Hornet PO10 36 C4
Horse Sands Cl PO4 30 C4
Horse La PO2 26 C1
Horsea Rd PO2 24 B6
Horsebridge Rd PO9 19 G2
Hoskins Ho PO1 4 B3
Hospital La PO16 22 D5
Houghton Cl PO9 15 H5
Howard Rd PO2 26 D1
Hoylake Rd PO6 25 E1
Hudson Rd PO5 5 H5
Hulbert Rd PO7 17 H1
Hunter Rd, Emsworth PO10 36 C4
Hunter Rd, Portsmouth PO6 24 B2
Hunter Rd, Southsea PO4 29 G4
Hunters Ride PO7 17 G2
Huntley Cl PO6 23 G2
Huntsman Cl PO8 11 B7
Hurn Ct PO9 15 H6
Hursley Rd PO9 18 D1
Hurst Green Cl PO9 14 B1
Hurstbourne Cl PO9 14 B6
Hurstville Dr PO7 17 H2
Hurstwood Av PO10 21 H5
Hussar Ct PO7 13 F6
Hyde Park Ho PO5 5 G3
Hyde Park Rd PO5 5 G3
Hyde St PO5 5 F5
Hylton Rd GU32 6 C5
Hythe Rd PO6 24 A2

Ibsley Gro PO9 18 C3
Icarus Pl PO7 17 H6
Idsworth Cl PO8 11 F6
Idsworth Down GU31 5 G1
Idsworth Rd, Portsmouth PO3 27 F5
Idsworth Rd, Waterlooville PO8 14 B2
Iford Ct PO9 15 H6
Ilex Walk PO11 33 E4
Ingledene Cl PO9 18 D4
Inglis Rd PO5 29 F4
Inhams La PO12 12 A2
Inhurst Av PO9 14 A3
Inhurst Rd PO2 26 B3
Inkpen Walk PO9 14 D5
Inmans La GU32 7 E2
Inner By-Pass PO10 20 D5
Invergordon Av PO6 25 E4
Inverness Rd PO1 26 D6
Iping Av PO9 18 D1
Ireland Way PO7 17 G4
Ironbridge La PO4 30 A3
Isambard Brunel Rd PO1 5 F2
Island Cl PO11 34 B4
Island View Ter PO2 26 B4
Island View Walk PO16 22 B2
Islay Gdns PO6 24 C2
Itchen Cl GU32 6 B6
Itchen Rd PO9 15 H6
Itchenor Rd PO11 33 G5
Ithica Cl PO11 32 C1
Ivy Ct PO7 17 F4
Ivy La PO1 4 C1
Ivy Orchard PO8 8 B2
Ivydene Gdns PO8 11 B8

Jack Cockerill PO5 29 E6
Jackdaw Cl PO8 13 G3
Jackson Cl PO6 25 F4
Jacobs Cl PO8 8 C3

Jacobs St PO1 5 G1
Jacqueline Av PO7 17 G5
Jade Ct*, London Rd PO7 17 G1
Jago Rd PO1 4 C1
James Callaghan Dr PO17 23 E1
James Cl PO11 32 A4
James Copse Rd PO8 11 A7
James Howell Ct PO7 12 C3
James Rd PO9 18 D3
Japonica Way PO9 19 H2
Jarndyce Walk PO2 26 B6
Jasmine Gro PO7 14 A6
Jasmine Way PO8 8 C3
Jasmond Rd PO6 24 C5
Jason Pl PO7 17 H6
Javelin Rd PO10 36 C4
Jay Cl PO8 11 C5
Jenkins Gro PO3 27 G6
Jersey Rd PO2 26 D5
Jervis Rd PO2 26 B3
Jessica Cl PO7 14 B3
Jessie Rd, Havant PO9 18 C3
Jessie Rd, Southsea PO4 29 F3
Jodrell Cl PO8 11 D5
John King Shipyard PO10 20 D6
Johns Ct*, Simpson Rd PO2 26 B4
Jolliffe Ct PO2 6 C5
Joseph Nye Ct PO1 4 D3
Jubilee Av PO6 22 D2
Jubilee Bsns Centre PO7 13 G6
Jubilee Ho, Emsworth PO10 20 B4
Jubilee Ho, Portsmouth PO6 24 B2
Jubilee Mews PO10 21 F6
Jubilee Rd, Fareham PO16 22 C3
Jubilee Rd, Southsea PO4 29 G4
Jubilee Rd, Waterlooville PO7 13 G6
Jubilee Ter*, East St PO10 5 E6
Juliet Ct PO7 14 B3
Juniper Rd PO8 10 E3
Jupiter Cl PO9 19 F5
Jupiter Ct PO1 4 C4
Jura Cl PO6 24 C2
Jute Cl PO16 22 A2
Juventu Cl PO9 19 F2

Karen Av PO6 25 E4
Kassassin St PO4 29 H5
Kassel Cl PO7 14 B3
Katkins Mews PO5 5 H6
Katrina Gdns PO11 32 C2
Kearsney Av PO2 26 D2
Keats Av PO6 22 D1
Keats Cl PO8 11 B7
Keats Ho PO9 19 E2
Keel Cl PO3 27 G2
Keelan Ct PO5 29 E5
Kefford Cl PO8 11 D6
Keith Ho PO1 4 D2
Kelly Rd PO7 17 G3
Kelsey Av PO10 21 H4
Kelsey Head PO6 23 F3
Kelvin Gro PO16 22 C2
Kempenfelt Ho PO1 4 D2
Kempton Pk PO7 14 B3
Kemshott Ct PO9 14 C5
Ken Berry Ct PO9 15 H6
Kenchester Cl PO6 23 H2
Kendal Av PO3 27 E4
Kendal Cl PO8 11 C7
Kenilworth Rd PO5 29 E6
Kennedy Cl PO7 17 G4
Kennet Rd GU32 6 B6
Kensington Rd PO2 27 E2
Kent Gro PO16 22 B5
Kent Rd PO5 28 D4
Kent St PO1 4 D3
Kentidge Rd PO7 17 F4
Kenwood Bsns Pk PO9 19 G3
Kenwood Rd PO16 22 G3
Kenya Rd PO16 22 A4
Kenyon Rd PO2 27 E3
Kestrel Cl PO8 8 C4
Kestrel Pl PO6 25 H4
Kestrel Rd PO3 27 F1
Keswick Av PO3 27 E4

Kettering Ter PO2 26 B
Keydell Av PO8 11 C
Keydell Cl PO8 11 C
Keyhaven Dr PO9 18 C
Khandala Gdns PO7 17 H
Kidmore La PO7 12 C
Kilbride Path PO2 26 C
Kilderkin Dr PO8 11 F
Kilmeston Cl PO9 15 E
Kilmiston Ct PO1 26 C
Kilmiston Dr PO16 22 B
Kiln Rd PO3 27 F
Kilnside PO7 12 C
Kilpatrick Cl PO2 26 C
Kilwich Way PO16 22 A
Kimberley Rd PO4 29 H
Kimbers GU32 6 C
Kimbolton Rd PO3 29 H
Kimbridge Cres PO9 15 G
Kimpton Ct PO9 15 H
King Albert St PO1 29 E
King Arthurs Ct PO6 25 F
King Charles St PO1 4 C
King Edwards Cres PO2 26 C
King George Av GU32 6 D
King George Rd PO16 22 C
King Henry I St PO1 5 F
King James Ter PO1 4 C
King John Av PO16 22 A
King Richard Cl PO8 23 H
King Richard I Rd PO1 5 E
King St, Emsworth PO10 20 D
King St, Southsea PO5 5 F
King St, Westbourne PO10 21 G
King William St PO1 4 D
Kingfisher Cl, Hayling Island PO11 33 E
Kingfisher Cl, Rowlands Castle PO9 9 B
Kingfisher Cl, Waterlooville PO8 13 G
Kingfisher Ct PO3 27 F
Kingfisher Dr PO10 21 F
Kings Bench Alley PO1 4 D
Kings Cl PO9 9 A
Kings Croft La PO9 18 C
Kings Mede PO8 11 C
Kings Mews PO5 29 E
Kings Rd, Emsworth PO10 20 B
Kings Rd, Hayling Island PO11 32 C
Kings Rd, Petersfield GU32 6 A
Kings Rd, Southsea PO5 5 E
Kings Rd, Waterlooville PO8 13 H
Kings Ter, Emsworth PO10 20 D
Kings Ter, Southsea PO5 5 E
Kingsclere Av PO9 14 D
Kingscote Rd, Portsmouth PO6 23 E
Kingscote Rd, Waterlooville PO8 13 F
Kingscroft Ct PO9 18 D
Kingsdown Pl PO1 29 F
Kingsdown Rd PO7 13 E
Kingsey Av PO10 20 B
Kingsfernsden La GU32 6 D
Kingsland Cl PO6 23 H
Kingsley Grn PO9 15 E
Kingsley Rd PO4 30 A
Kingston Cres PO2 26 C
Kingston Rd PO2 26 C
Kingsway PO11 34 B
Kingswell St PO1 5 F
Kingsworthy Rd PO9 19 E
Kinnell Ct PO10 20 C
Kinross Cres PO6 24 D
Kintyre Rd PO6 24 C
Kipling Rd PO2 26 D
Kirby Rd PO2 26 D
Kirkstall Rd PO4 29 F
Kirpal Rd PO3 30 A
Kirton Rd PO6 25 E
Kite Cl PO8 13 G
Kitwood Grn*, Bartons Rd PO8 19 H
Knight Gdns PO6 25 G
Knightwood Av PO9 19 G
Knowsley Cres PO6 24 C
Knowsley Rd PO6 24 C

Knox Rd, Havant PO9 18 D4
Knox Rd, Portsmouth PO2 26 B4
Kyoto Ter PO9 19 G2

Laburnum Av PO6 25 E3
Laburnum Gro, Hayling Island PO11 32 D3
Laburnum Gro, Portsmouth PO2 26 C4
Laburnum Rd PO7 17 G3
Ladybridge Rd PO7 17 E5
Ladyward Ho PO5 5 G4
Lake Rd PO1 5 H1
Lakeside Av PO3 27 F6
Lakeside Gdns PO9 19 F3
Lakesmere Rd PO8 11 D6
Lambert Cl PO7 17 G4
Lampeter Av PO6 24 D3
Lancaster Cl PO16 22 A2
Lancaster Way PO7 17 H2
Landguard Rd PO4 29 H4
Landport St, Portsmouth PO1 5 H1
Landport St, Southsea PO5 5 E5
Landport Ter PO1 5 E5
Landport Vw PO1 5 G1
Lane End Dr PO9 20 C5
Langbrook Cl PO9 19 E6
Langdale Av PO6 24 D4
Langford Rd PO1 26 D5
Langley Cotts PO10 21 F6
Langley Rd PO2 26 D5
Langrish Cl PO9 15 G6
Langstone Av PO9 34 A1
Langstone High St PO9 34 A1
Langstone Ho PO9 19 G2
Langstone Rd, Langstone PO9 34 A1
Langstone Rd, Portsmouth PO9 29 H1
Langstone Technology Pk PO9 19 E6
Lansdown Av PO16 22 C5
Lansdowne Av PO7 16 D6
Lansdowne St PO5 5 E5
Lantana Cl PO7 17 H3
Lapwing Cl PO8 11 C5
Lapwing Rd PO4 30 B2
Larchfield Way PO8 11 D7
Larchwood Av PO9 18 B2
Larcombe Rd GU32 6 B6
Lark Way PO10 21 F2
Larkhill Rd PO3 27 E1
Larkwhistle Walk PO9 14 C5
Lasham Grn PO9 15 G6
Lashly Mdw PO7 9 B2
Latchmore Forest Gro PO8 11 B8
Latchmore Gdns PO8 11 A8
Latimer Ct PO3 27 G1
Lauder Cl PO10 21 G4
Laurel Rd PO8 11 D7
Lauren Mews PO11 32 A5
Laurence Grn PO10 20 D2
Laurus Cl PO7 14 A6
Lavant Cl PO8 14 B2
Lavant Ct GU32 6 C4
Lavant Dr PO9 19 F3
Lavant St GU32 6 C4
Lavender Rd PO7 14 A5
Laverock Lea PO16 22 B2
Lawnswood Av PO8 13 H4
Lawrence Cl PO8 13 G4
Lawrence Rd PO5 29 F4
Lawson Rd PO5 29 F3
Lazy Acre PO10 21 G5
Lealand Gro PO6 25 F3
Lealand Rd PO6 24 D6
Leamington Ho PO5 5 F4
Leckford Cl PO16 22 B1
Leckford PO9 15 G6
Ledbury Rd PO6 23 G2
Legion Rd PO11 32 C3
Leigh Rd PO9 19 F4
Leith Av PO16 22 C2
Lendorber Av PO6 24 C3
Lennox Lodge PO11 32 A4
Lennox Rd North PO5 29 E5
Lennox Rd South PO5 29 E5
Lennox Row PO1 4 D1
Lensyd Gdns PO8 11 B6
Leofric Ct PO4 30 B4
Leominster Rd PO9 23 G1
Leopold St PO4 29 F5
Lester Av PO9 18 C4
Lewis Rd PO10 20 D3

Lexden Gdns PO11 32 B3
Liam Cl PO9 19 F1
Library Gdns PO9 19 E3
Lichfield Rd PO3 29 H1
Liddiards Way PO7 17 G6
Lidiard Gdns PO4 30 A5
Lightfoot Lawn PO4 30 B4
Lilac Cl PO9 19 H2
Limberline Rd PO3 24 C6
Limberline Spur PO3 24 C6
Lime Gro, Hayling Island PO11 31 G4
Lime Gro, Portsmouth PO6 23 G1
Lincoln Rd PO1 29 F2
Lincoln Rise PO8 11 C8
Lind Cl PO7 17 H5
Linda Gro PO8 11 A8
Linden Gro PO11 32 C4
Linden Lea PO16 22 A2
Linden Way, Havant PO9 19 F2
Linden Way, Waterlooville PO8 11 D6
Lindens Cl PO10 20 C3
Lindisfarne Cl PO4 24 C3
Lindley Av PO4 29 H5
Linford Ct PO1 14 D5
Lingfield Ct PO1 5 E6
Link Rd, Fareham PO17 23 G1
Link Rd, Havant PO9 18 C2
Linkenholt Way PO8 18 C1
Links Cl PO9 9 B6
Links La, Hayling Island PO11 31 G4
Links La, Rowlands Castle PO9 9 B5
Linnet Cl, Petersfield GU31 7 G5
Linnet Cl, Waterlooville PO8 13 G2
Lion St PO1 5 E2
Lion Ter PO1 5 E2
Lisle Way PO10 20 B2
Liss Rd PO4 29 G3
Lister Rd PO6 24 B2
Lith Av PO8 10 D3
Lith Cres PO8 10 D3
Lith La PO8 10 E3
Little Arthur St PO2 26 C6
Little Cnr PO7 12 C4
Little George St PO1 26 D6
Little Hambrook St PO5 5 F6
Little Hyden La PO8 8 B1
Little Mead PO7 12 C4
Little Southsea St PO5 5 F6
Littlegreen Av PO9 19 G2
Littlepark Av PO9 18 B3
Littleton Gro PO9 19 F1
Liverpool Rd PO1 29 F2
Livesay Gdns PO3 29 G1
Livingstone Rd PO5 29 F4
Lobelia Ct PO7 14 A6
Locarno Rd PO3 27 E3
Lock App PO6 23 F4
Lock Vw PO6 23 F4
Lockerley Rd PO9 19 F2
Locksheath Cl PO9 14 D6
Locksway Rd PO4 29 H3
Lodge Av PO6 24 D3
Lodge Rd PO9 18 B5
Lodgebury Cl PO10 21 H5
Lodsworth Cl PO8 8 D4
Lombard Cl PO1 4 C5
Lombard St PO1 4 C5
Lombardy Rise PO7 17 H4
Lomond Cl PO2 26 D6
Londesborough Rd PO4 29 F4
London Av PO2 26 C3
London Rd, Catherington PO8 10 E3
London Rd, Cosham PO6 24 C3
London Rd, Cowplain PO8 11 C8
London Rd, Petersfield GU31 7 F2
London Rd, Portsmouth PO2 24 B5
London Rd, Waterlooville PO7 17 E6
Lone Valley PO7 17 F6
Long Acre Ct PO9 26 D6
Long Copse Ct PO10 20 D1
Long Copse La PO10 20 C1
Long Curtain Rd PO5 28 B4
Long Down GU32 7 E3

Long Rd GU32 6 D2
Longbridge Ho PO5 5 F4
Longdean Cl PO6 23 F2
Longfield Cl PO4 30 A2
Longfield Rd PO10 20 C2
Longlands Rd PO10 21 G6
Longmead Ct PO9 19 F6
Longmead Gdns PO9 19 F6
Longs Walk PO1 5 H6
Longshore Way PO4 30 C3
Longstock Rd PO9 15 G6
Longwood Av PO8 11 A8
Lonsdale Av, Fareham PO16 22 C5
Lonsdale Av, Portsmouth PO6 24 C4
Lord Montgomery Way PO1 5 E4
Lordington Cl PO6 25 E3
Lords St PO1 29 E1
Lorne Rd PO5 29 F3
Louis Flagg Ho PO5 5 G5
Lovage Way PO8 10 E3
Love La GU31 6 D4
Lovedean La PO8 10 A4
Lovett Rd PO3 27 E2
Lowcay Rd PO5 29 E5
Lower Bere Wood PO7 17 H2
Lower Brookfield Rd PO1 29 F1
Lower Church Path PO1 5 G2
Lower Derby Rd PO2 26 B4
Lower Drayton La PO6 25 E4
Lower Farlington Rd PO6 25 G3
Lower Farm Dr PO6 24 A4
Lower Forbury Rd PO5 5 H4
Lower Grove Rd PO9 19 F5
Lower Heyshott La PO8 6 D4
Lower Mead GU31 7 F4
Lower Rd PO9 18 B5
Lower Wardown GU32 7 E4
Lower Wingfield St PO1 29 E1
Lowestoft Rd PO6 24 A2
Lowland Rd PO7 12 B2
Loxwood Rd PO8 11 B5
Luard Ct PO9 19 H5
Lucerne Av PO7 13 F5
Lucknow St PO1 29 F2
Ludcombe PO7 12 C2
Ludlow Rd PO6 23 G2
Lugano Cl PO7 13 F5
Luker Dr GU31 6 D3
Lulworth Cl PO11 32 C2
Lumley Gdns PO10 20 D5
Lumley Path PO10 20 D5
Lumley Rd PO10 20 D5
Lumsden Rd PO4 30 C4
Lutman St PO10 20 D4
Luxor Pk PO9 19 E6
Lychgate Dr PO8 10 C4
Lydney Cl PO6 23 H3
Lymbourn Rd PO9 19 G5
Lynden Cl PO11 32 A3
Lyndhurst Rd PO11 32 C5
Lyndhurst Rd PO2 26 D3
Lyndum Cl GU32 6 C4
Lyne Pl PO8 11 C6
Lynn Rd PO2 26 D5
Lynton Gro PO3 27 F5
Lynton Rd PO3 6 B3
Lynwood Av PO8 13 F4
Lysander Ct PO1 4 C4
Lysander Way PO7 14 A4

Maitland St PO1 26 C6
Maldon Rd PO6 24 A2
Malins Rd PO2 26 C6
Mallard Rd, Rowlands Castle PO9 9 A6
Mallard Rd, Southsea PO4 30 A2
Mallard Way PO10 21 F2
Mallow Cl PO7 14 A5
Mallow Cl*, London Rd PO6 24 C3
Malmesbury Lawn PO9 14 C6
Malta Rd PO2 26 D5
Malthouse Rd PO6 26 C5
Malvern Mews PO10 20 D5
Malvern Rd PO5 29 E5
Malwood Cl PO9 15 G5
Manchester Rd PO1 29 F2
Manchester Ter PO10 21 E2
Manners La PO4 29 F3
Manners Rd PO4 29 F3
Manor Cl PO9 19 F4
Manor Cres PO6 24 A5
Manor Ct PO9 18 D5
Manor Gdns PO10 21 G5
Manor Lodge Rd PO9 9 A6
Manor Mews PO6 25 E3
Manor Park Av PO3 27 E5
Manor Rd, Emsworth PO10 21 G5
Manor Rd, Hayling Island PO11 32 B3
Manor Rd, Portsmouth PO1 26 D6
Manor Way, Emsworth PO10 21 G5
Manor Way, Hayling Island PO11 32 C5
Mansion Rd PO4 29 F6
Mansvid Av PO6 24 D4
Mantle Sq PO2 26 A3
Maple Cl PO10 20 D3
Maple Cres PO8 8 D3
Maple Ct PO11 32 A3
Maple Dr PO7 12 D3
Maple Rd PO5 29 E5
Maple Wood PO9 18 B4
Mapletree Av PO8 11 D7
Mapletree Cl PO8 11 D7
Maralyn Av PO7 17 G2
Marazan Rd PO3 27 F3
Marchwood Rd PO9 15 E5
Marden Way GU31 6 D4
Margaret Cl PO9 13 F5
Margate Rd PO5 5 H5
Margerys Ct PO1 4 D3
Marie Ct*, London Rd PO7 17 G1
Marina Cl PO10 20 D6
Marina Gro, Fareham PO16 22 B4
Marina Gro, Portsmouth PO3 27 G6
Marina Keep PO6 23 F4
Marine Ct PO4 29 H5
Marine Walk PO11 33 E4
Mariners Walk PO4 30 A2
Marion Rd PO4 29 F5
Marjoram Cres PO8 11 D8
Mark Anthony Ct PO11 32 B4
Mark Cl PO3 27 E1
Mark Ct PO7 13 G6
Market Par PO9 19 F4
Marketway PO1 5 F1
Markway Cl PO10 20 B5
Marlands Lawn PO9 14 C6
Marlborough Av PO1 4 C3
Marlborough Cl PO7 17 F3
Marlborough Gro PO16 22 B4
Marlborough Pk PO9 19 H3
Marlborough Row PO1 4 C1
Marldell Cl PO9 15 G6
Marlowe Ct PO7 13 G5
Marmion Av PO5 29 E5
Marmion Rd PO5 28 D5
Marples Way PO9 18 D5
Marrels Wood PO7 17 E4
Marsden Rd PO6 23 G3
Marsh Cl PO6 25 E5
Marshall Rd PO11 33 E5
Marshfield Ho PO6 25 F4
Marshlands Rd PO6 25 G4
Marshlands Spur PO6 25 G4
Marshwood Av PO7 14 A4
Marston La PO3 27 G1

Martells Ct PO1 4 D4
Martin Av PO7 12 C2
Martin Rd, Havant PO9 19 F1
Martin Rd, Portsmouth PO3 27 F5
Marvic Ct PO9 15 E6
Mary Rose Ho PO9 14 C5
Masefield Av PO6 23 E2
Masefield Cres PO8 11 A8
Masons Walk PO7 12 A2
Matapan Rd PO2 26 C1
Matthews Cl PO9 18 C3
Maurepas Way PO7 17 G1
Maurice Rd PO4 30 A3
Mavis Cres PO9 19 E4
Maxwell Rd PO4 29 H4
Maydman Sq PO3 29 H1
Mayfield Rd PO2 26 D3
Mayflower Dr PO4 30 B2
Mayhall Rd PO3 27 E4
Maylands Av PO6 29 H2
Maylands Rd PO9 18 B3
Mayles Rd PO4 30 A2
Maynard Pl PO8 10 C4
Mayo Cl PO1 26 C6
Maytree Gdns PO8 13 G4
Maytree Rd PO8 13 G4
Mead End Rd PO7 12 C4
Meadend Cl PO9 15 H6
Meadow Cl PO11 35 B5
Meadow Ct PO10 20 D5
Meadow Edge PO7 24 D1
Meadow Rise PO8 11 C8
Meadow St PO5 5 F5
Meadow Walk PO1 5 F1
Meadowlands, Havant PO9 19 G5
Meadowlands, Rowlands Castle PO9 9 B5
Meadowsweet PO7 14 B2
Meadowsweet Way PO6 24 A1
Meadway PO7 14 A3
Meath Cl PO11 33 E6
Medina Rd PO6 24 A3
Medstead Rd PO9 19 E2
Melbourne Ho PO1 5 H2
Melbourne St PO5 5 F4
Mellor Cl PO6 24 A3
Melrose Cl PO4 30 A3
Melville Rd PO4 30 B5
Mengham Av PO11 32 C5
Mengham Cl PO11 32 C4
Mengham La PO11 32 C4
Mengham Rd PO11 32 C4
Menslands La PO7 9 A3
Meon Cl, Petersfield GU32 6 B4
Meon Cl, Waterlooville PO8 8 D4
Meon Cl, Southsea PO4 29 H3
Meon Rd, Southsea PO4 30 A2
Mercator Av PO1 4 C4
Merchants Row PO1 4 C5
Merchistoun Rd PO8 11 C5
Mercury Pl PO7 17 G6
Meredith Rd PO2 26 D2
Meriden Rd PO5 5 F4
Meridian Centre PO9 19 F4
Merlin Cl PO8 11 A7
Merlin Dr PO3 27 E1
Merlin Gdns PO16 22 A2
Merritts Farm Cotts PO7 12 D2
Merrivale Ct PO10 21 G4
Merrivale Rd PO2 26 D2
Merrow Cl PO16 22 A3
Merryfield Av PO9 14 D6
Merryfield Rd GU32 7 E3
Merthyr Av PO6 25 E2
Merton Av PO16 22 C5
Merton Cres PO16 22 C5
Merton Rd PO5 28 D5
Meryl Rd PO4 30 B3
Meteor Rd PO10 36 C4
Methuen Rd PO4 29 H4
Mewsey Ct PO9 14 D5
Mey Cl PO7 14 A6
Meyrick Rd, Bedhampton PO9 18 D4
Meyrick Rd, Portsmouth PO2 26 B4
Michael Crook Cl PO9 18 D5
Midas Cl PO7 17 H5
Middle Park Way PO9 14 C4
Middle St PO5 5 F5

Middlesex Rd PO4 29 H3
Middleton Rise PO8 8 D4
Midway Rd PO2 24 B6
Milbeck Cl PO8 11 C8
Mile End Rd PO2 26 B6
Milebush Rd PO4 30 A2
Miles Ct PO11 33 F6
Milford Cl PO9 18 D2
Milford Rd PO1 5 H2
Military Rd, Landport PO1 26 A6
Military Rd, Portsmouth PO3 24 B6
Mill Cl, Hayling Island PO11 35 B5
Mill Cl, Waterlooville PO7 12 D3
Mill End PO10 21 E5
Mill La, Emsworth PO10 20 D4
Mill La, Havant PO9 18 C5
Mill La, Langstone PO9 34 A1
Mill La, Petersfield GU32 7 E1
Mill La, Portsmouth PO1 26 B6
Mill La, Waterlooville PO7 16 B5
Mill Quay PO10 21 E6
Mill Rd, Denmead PO7 12 D3
Mill Rd, Emsworth PO10 21 E1
Mill Rd, Purbrook PO7 17 F3
Mill Rythe La PO11 35 C8
Millbrook Dr PO9 15 G6
Millennium Ct PO7 17 G3
Mills Rd PO2 26 C4
Milton Ct PO4 29 H2
Milton La PO4 29 G2
Milton Par PO8 13 G4
Milton Park Av PO4 29 H3
Milton Rd, Portsmouth PO3 27 E6
Milton Rd, Waterlooville PO7,8 13 F6
Milverton Ho PO5 5 G5
Minerva Cl PO7 17 G6
Minerva Cres PO1 4 C4
Minley Ct PO9 19 H1
Minstead Rd PO4 30 A4
Minters Lepe PO7 17 G6
Mission La PO8 14 A1
Mitchell Rd PO9 18 B2
Mitchell Way PO3 27 G2
Mizen Ho PO6 23 F4
Moggs Mead GU31 6 D4
Mole Hill PO7 17 H3
Monarch Cl PO7 14 A4
Monckton Rd PO3 27 E3
Moneyfield Av PO3 27 F4
Moneyfield La PO3 27 F5
Monks Hill PO10 21 E1
Monks Orchard GU32 6 C2
Monkwood Cl PO9 14 D6
Monmouth Rd PO2 26 C3
Montague Gdns GU31 7 F4
Montague Rd PO2 26 C3
Montague Wallis Ct PO1 4 D3
Montana Ct PO7 14 A6
Monterey Dr PO9 19 G1
Montgomerie Rd PO5 5 H4
Montgomery Rd PO9 19 F4
Montgomery Walk PO7 17 F3
Montrose Av PO16 22 D2
Monxton Grn*, Burghclere Rd PO9 15 H6
Moor Pk PO7 14 B2
Moorgreen Rd PO9 19 G1
Moorings Way PO4 30 A2
Moorland Rd PO1 29 F1
Moortown Av PO6 25 F2
Moraunt Dr PO16 22 A4
Morecambe Ct PO5 5 H4
Morelands Ct PO7 17 H5
Morelands Rd PO7 17 G5
Morgan Rd PO4 30 A3
Morley Cres PO8 11 B8
Morley Rd PO4 29 H5
Morningside Av PO16 22 D2
Mortimer Lawn PO9 14 D5
Mortimer Rd PO6 23 G2
Mosdell Rd PO10 21 H6
Moulin Av PO5 29 F5
Mountbatten Bsns Pk PO6 25 F5
Mountbatten Dr PO7 17 F3
Mountbatten Sq PO4 30 A5
Mountbatten Way PO1 26 A6
Mountjoy Ct PO1 4 C6
Mountview Av PO16 22 D2
Mountwood Rd PO10 21 G4
Mousehole Rd PO6 23 E2
Muccleshell Cl PO9 19 G2
Mulberry Av PO6 24 D3
Mulberry La PO6 24 C3
Mulberry Path PO6 24 D3
Mullion Cl PO6 23 G4
Mundays Row PO8 10 D3
Munster Rd PO2 26 C3
Murefield Rd PO1 29 E2
Muriel Rd PO7 13 G6
Murray Rd PO8 11 D6
Murrills Est PO16 22 D3
Muscliffe Ct PO9 15 H6
Museum Rd PO1 5 E5
My Lords La PO11 32 D4
Myrtle Av PO16 22 C4
Myrtle Gro PO3 27 G6

Nailsworth Rd PO6 23 G2
Naish Ct PO9 14 C5
Nancy Rd PO1 29 F2
Napier Rd, Southsea PO5 29 E5
Napier Rd, Waterlooville PO8 11 D5
Narvik Rd PO2 26 C1
Naseby Cl PO6 23 F2
Navy Rd PO1 28 B1
Neelands Gro PO6 22 D3
Nelson Av, Fareham PO16 22 A3
Nelson Av, Portsmouth PO2 26 C2
Nelson Cres PO8 11 D5
Nelson Dr GU31 6 D3
Nelson La PO17 22 B1
Nelson Rd PO1 26 C6
Neptune Ct PO1 4 C4
Nerissa Cl PO7 14 B3
Nessus St PO2 26 C5
Nest Bsns Pk PO9 19 G1
Netherfield Cl PO9 19 G5
Netley Rd PO5 28 D5
Netley Ter PO5 28 D5
Nettlecombe Av PO4 29 F6
Nettlestone Rd PO4 29 H5
Neville Av PO16 22 C5
Neville Gdns PO10 20 B2
Neville Rd PO3 27 F6
Neville Shute Rd PO3 27 F2
New Brighton Rd PO10 20 D4
New Cut PO11 34 B4
New Down La, Cosham PO7 16 C6
New Down La, Purbrook PO7 16 D5
New Down La, Widley PO7 24 D1
New La PO9 19 G4
New Rd, Clanfield PO8 8 C4
New Rd, Havant PO9 18 D4
New Rd, Horndean PO8 11 A5
New Rd, Portsmouth PO2 26 D6
New Rd, Southbourne PO10 21 H6
New Rd, Westbourne PO10 21 E2
New Rd East PO2 27 E5
Newbarn Rd PO9 18 B2
Newbolt Cl PO8 11 A8
Newbolt Rd PO6 22 D2
Newcome Rd PO1 29 F1
Newcomen Ct*, Newcomen Rd PO2 26 B3
Newcomen Rd PO2 26 B3
Newham Ct PO9 15 G6
Newlands La PO7 12 B5
Newlands Rd PO7 17 F4
Newlease Rd PO7 17 H4
Newlyn Way PO6 23 F4
Newmer Ct PO9 14 C5
Newney Cl PO2 27 E1
Newtown PO16 22 C3
Newtown La PO11 32 A3
Nicholas Ct*, Seafront PO11 32 A4
Nicholson Gdns PO1 5 H1
Nicholson Way PO9 19 E3
Nickel St PO5 5 E6
Nickleby Rd PO8 8 C2
Nightingale Cl PO9 9 A6
Nightingale Pk PO9 19 H5
Nightingale Rd, Petersfield GU32 6 B6
Nightingale Rd, Southsea PO5 28 D5
Nightjar Cl PO8 11 C5
Nile St PO10 20 D6
Ninian Park Rd PO3 27 F3
Ninian Path PO3 27 F3
Nobbs La PO1 4 D5
Nore Cres PO10 20 A5
Nore Farm Av PO10 20 B5
Noreuil Rd GU32 6 B4
Norfolk Cres PO11 32 A5
Norfolk Mews PO11 32 A5
Norfolk St PO5 5 F5
Norgett Way PO16 22 B4
Norland Rd PO4 29 F4
Norley Cl PO9 19 E1
Norman Cl PO16 22 C5
Norman Ct PO4 29 F5
Norman Rd, Hayling Island PO11 32 D5
Norman Rd, Southsea PO4 29 F4
Norman Way PO9 18 C4
Normandy Rd PO2 26 C1
Norris Gdns PO9 19 G5
North Av PO2 24 B6
North Battery Rd PO2 26 A3
North Bay PO10 36 C4
North Brook Cl PO1 26 C6
North Cl PO9 19 G5
North Cres PO11 32 D5
North End Av PO2 26 C3
North End Gro PO2 26 C3
North Grove Ho PO5 5 H6
North La PO8 8 B2
North Rd, Fareham PO17 23 G1
North Rd, Petersfield GU32 6 D3
North Rd, Waterlooville PO8 10 E2
North Shore Rd PO11 31 H3
North St, Bedhampton PO9 18 D4
North St, Emsworth PO10 20 D4
North St, Havant PO9 19 F4
North St, Portsmouth PO1 4 D2
North St, Westbourne PO10 21 E1
Northam Mews PO1 5 H2
Northam St PO1 5 H1
Northarbour Rd PO6 23 H3
Northarbour Spur PO6 23 H3
Northcote Gdns PO10 21 H5
Northcote Rd PO4 29 F4
Northern Par PO2 26 C2
Northern Rd PO6 24 B5
Northfield Cl PO8 10 E2
Northfield Pk PO16 22 A2
Northgate Av PO2 27 E5
Northney La PO11 34 D3
Northney Rd PO11 34 B3
Northover Rd PO3 27 F5
Northumberland Rd PO5 29 F2
Northway PO9 19 E4
Northwood La PO11 35 B6
Northwood Rd PO2 24 B6
Norton Cl PO7 17 G2
Norway Rd PO3 27 E1
Norwich Rd PO6 24 A2
Novello Gdns PO7 17 G3
Nursery Cl PO10 20 D2
Nursery Gdns PO8 11 B7
Nursery Rd PO9 18 C4
Nursling Cres PO9 15 G6
Nutbourne Rd, Hayling Island PO11 33 G5
Nutbourne Rd, Portsmouth PO6 25 F4
Nutfield Pl PO1 29 E1
Nuthatch Cl PO9 9 B6
Nutley Rd PO9 14 D6
Nutwick Rd PO9 19 H2
Nyewood Av PO16 22 C1

O'Jays Ind Pk PO3 27 F3
Oak Cl PO8 13 G4
Oak Pk Dr PO9 19 G3
Oak Pk Ind Est PO6 23 H3
Oak Rd PO8 8 D3
Oak Tree Dr PO10 20 C1
Oakapple Gdns PO6 25 H2
Oakdene Rd PO4 30 B3
Oakfield Ct PO9 15 H6
Oakhurst Dr PO7 14 A4
Oakhurst Gdns PO7 24 D1
Oaklands Gro PO8 13 G3
Oaklands Rd, Havant PO9 19 G5
Oaklands Rd, Petersfield GU32 6 C3
Oaklea Cl PO7 24 D1
Oakley Ho PO5 5 G6
Oakley Rd PO9 18 D1
Oakmeadow Cl PO10 20 D2
Oakmont Dr PO8 13 H5
Oaks Coppice PO8 11 C6
Oakshott Dr PO9 15 G6
Oakum Ho PO3 29 G1
Oakwood Av PO9 18 B3
Oakwood Rd, Hayling Island PO11 32 B4
Oakwood Rd, Portsmouth PO2 26 D1
Oberon Cl PO7 14 A4
Ocean Ct*, Magdala Rd PO11 32 A4
Ocean Pk Shopping Centre PO3 27 F3
Octavius Ct PO7 14 B3
Old Barn Cres PO7 9 B3
Old Barn Gdns PO8 11 A6
Old Bridge Rd PO4 29 F5
Old Canal PO4 30 A3
Old Commercial Rd PO1 26 B6
Old Copse Rd PO9 19 F3
Old Farm La PO10 21 E3
Old Farm Way PO6 25 G3
Old Gate Gdns PO2 26 D1
Old La PO8 10 C2
Old London Rd PO2 27 E1
Old Manor Way PO6 24 D4
Old Market Rd PO6 24 C3
Old Mill La GU31 7 F2
Old Rectory Cl PO10 21 E2
Old Rectory Rd PO6 25 H2
Old Reservoir Rd PO6 25 F4
Old River PO7 12 C3
Old School Dr PO11 32 D5
Old Star Pl PO1 4 C2
Old Timbers PO11 32 B4
Old Van Diemans Rd PO7 17 F4
Old Wymering La PO6 24 A3
Oldbury Ho PO5 5 F4
Olinda St PO1 29 F1
Olive Cres PO16 22 C4
Oliver Rd PO4 29 G4
Olivia Cl PO7 14 B3
Omega Ho PO5 5 H3
Omega St PO5 5 H3
Onslow Rd PO5 29 E6
Ophir Rd PO2 26 C2
Oracle Dr PO7 17 G6
Orange Row PO10 20 D6
Orchard Cl, Hayling Island PO11 32 B5
Orchard Cl, Waterlooville PO8 11 E5
Orchard Gro, Fareham PO16 22 A4
Orchard Gro, Waterlooville PO8 13 H4
Orchard La PO10 21 E5
Orchard Rd, Havant PO9 19 F5
Orchard Rd, Hayling Island PO11 32 C5
Orchard Rd, Southsea PO4 29 F3
Ordnance Ct PO3 24 D6
Ordnance Row PO1 4 C3
Orford Ct*, Magdala Rd PO6 24 C3
Oriel Rd PO2 26 C3
Orkney Rd PO6 24 C2
Ormsby Rd PO5 28 D4
Orsmond Cl PO7 17 H3
Orwell Rd GU32 6 B6
Osborne Cl PO7 14 A4
Osborne Rd, Petersfield GU32 6 C4
Osborne Rd, Southsea PO5 28 D5
Osier Cl PO2 26 B2
Osier Rd GU32 6 B5
Osprey Cl PO6 25 H3
Osprey Dr PO11 32 D4
Osprey Quay PO10 36 C1
Othello Dr PO7 14 A4
Otterbourne Cres PO9 18 D1
Outram Rd PO5 5 H6
Overton Cres PO9 18 D1
Overton Rd PO10 21 H4
Owen Ho PO3 29 G1
Owen St PO4 29 H5
Owslebury Gro PO9 19 F1
Oxenwood Grn PO9 14 D6
Oxford Rd PO5 29 F4
Oxted Ct PO4 30 A2
Oyster Mews PO1 4 C5
Oyster Quay PO6 23 G4
Oyster St PO1 4 C6

Padbury Cl PO2 27 E1
Paddington Rd PO2 27 E4
Paddock End PO7 12 C3
Paddock Walk PO6 23 F3
Paddock Way GU32 6 B6
Padnell Av PO8 14 A1
Padnell Pl PO8 14 B1
Padnell Rd PO8 14 A1
Padwick Av PO6 24 C3
Padwick Ct*, Green La PO11 32 A4
Pagham Cl PO10 20 D5
Pagham Gdns PO11 33 H5
Paignton Av PO3 27 F5
Pains Rd PO5 5 H4
Painswick Cl PO6 23 H3
Painter Cl PO3 27 G2
Palk Rd PO9 18 D4
Palm Ct PO5 28 D5
Palmers Rd PO10 20 D5
Palmers Rd Ind Est PO10 20 D5
Palmerston Rd, Hayling Island PO11 32 C3
Palmerston Rd, Southsea PO5 28 D5
Palmerston Rd Precinct PO5 28 D5
Pamela Av PO6 23 E2
Pan St PO1 5 G1
Pangbourne Av PO6 24 D4
Panton Cl PO10 20 C2
Parade Ct PO2 24 B6
Paradise La PO10 21 E1
Paradise St PO1 5 G2
Park Av PO7 17 E6
Park Cres PO10 20 B5
Park Ct PO5 5 F6
Park Farm Rd PO7 17 F5
Park Gro PO6 24 C4
Park House Farm Way PO9 18 B1
Park La, Bedhampton PO9 18 C3
Park La, Havant PO9 14 C4
Park La, Portsmouth PO6 24 C3
Park La, Waterlooville PO7,8 14 A1
Park Par PO9 19 E1
Park Rd, Denmead PO7 12 B2
Park Rd, Emsworth PO10 21 G5
Park Rd, Hayling Island PO11 31 H3
Park Rd, Petersfield GU32 6 C4
Park Rd, Portsmouth PO1 4 D3
Park Rd, Purbrook PO7 17 E5
Park Rd North PO9 19 E4
Park Rd South PO9 19 E5
Park Royal PO2 26 D1
Park Side PO9 18 C3
Park St PO5 5 F4
Park View Ct PO9 15 H3
Park Way PO9 19 E4
Parker Gdns PO7 17 F6
Parklands Av PO8 11 B7
Parklands Bsns Pk PO7 12 B4
Parkstone Av PO4 29 F6
Parkstone La PO4 29 F5
Parkwood Centre PO7 17 G1
Parr Rd PO6 24 A3
Parry Cl PO6 22 D3
Parsons Cl PO3 24 C6

Partridge Gdns PO8 13 F2
Passfield Walk*,
Bartons PO9 19 H1
Passingham Walk PO8 11 B7
Pasteur Rd PO6 24 B2
Patrick Howard PO8 11 A7
Paulsgrove Enterprise Centre PO6 23 G2
Paulsgrove Ind Centre PO6 23 G3
Paulsgrove Rd PO2 26 D4
Peacock La PO1 4 D5
Peak Rd PO8 8 B3
Peakfield PO7 12 B3
Pebble Cl PO11 32 D5
Pebble Ct PO11 33 F6
Pebmarsh Rd PO6 24 A3
Pedam Cl PO4 29 H4
Peel PI PO5 5 F4
Pelham Rd PO5 5 G6
Pelham Ter PO10 20 D6
Pembroke Cl PO1 4 D6
Pembroke Rd PO1 4 D6
Pembury Rd PO9 19 G5
Penarth Av PO6 25 E3
Pendennis Rd PO6 23 E2
Penhale Rd PO1 29 F2
Penhurst Rd PO9 18 B3
Penjar Av PO7 17 E5
Penk Ridge PO9 25 H2
Pennant Hills PO9 18 B4
Penner Rd PO9 18 D6
Pennerly Ct PO9 14 D4
Penns PI GU31 7 G4
Penns Rd GU32 6 C3
Penny La PO10 21 F6
Penny PI PO7 17 G5
Penny St PO1 4 C6
Penrhyn Av PO6 25 E3
Penrose Cl PO2 26 C3
Pentere Rd PO8 11 B5
Pentland Rise PO16 22 C2
Penton Ct PO9 15 H6
Penwood Grn*,
Minley PO9 19 H1
Peper Harow PO8 11 C6
Pepys Cl PO4 29 G4
Percival Rd PO2 27 E5
Percy Chandler St PO1 5 H1
Percy Rd PO4 29 F3
Peronne Cl PO3 24 C6
Peronne Rd PO3 24 B6
Perseus PI PO7 17 H6
Perseus Ter PO1 4 C4
Perth Ho PO1 5 H2
Perth Rd PO4 30 A3
Pervin Rd PO6 24 C3
Peter Ashley La PO6 25 F2
Peterborough Rd PO6 24 A2
Petersfield Bsns Pk GU32 6 B5
Petersfield By-Pass GU32 6 A6
Petersfield Ho PO1 5 H1
Petersfield Rd, Havant PO9 19 E3
Petersfield Rd, Waterlooville PO8 8 C2
Petersham Cl PO7 13 F5
Petworth Rd PO3 29 H1
Philip Av PO1 4 C3
Philip Rd PO7 17 H3
Phoenix Bldgs PO3 27 F3
Phoenix Sq PO2 26 D1
Picton Ho PO5 5 G4
Pier Head Rd PO2 26 A4
Pier Rd PO5 5 E6
Pigeon House La PO7 16 A3
Pine Ct PO10 20 C2
Pine Dr PO8 8 D3
Pine Gro PO9 19 G5
Pine Tree Gdns PO8 14 A1
Pinehurst Cl PO7 14 C2
Pinewood Av PO9 18 B3
Pink Rd PO2 26 D5
Pipers Mead PO8 8 B3
Pipers Wood Ind Pk PO7 13 E6
Pipit Cl PO8 11 C5
Pitcairn Mews PO4 30 A5
Pitcroft Rd PO2 26 C4
Pitreavie Rd PO6 24 C5
Place Cres PO7 17 H4
Plaitford Gro PO9 18 B1
Playfair Rd PO5 5 H4
Pleasant La PO1 37 E2
Pleasant Rd PO4 30 A3
Plover Reach PO4 30 A2

Plovers Rd PO8 11 C5
Plumley Walk PO9 14 D4
Plumpton Gdns PO3 27 G1
Plumpton Gro PO7 14 B3
Plymouth St PO5 5 G3
Pompey Centre PO4 29 G2
Pompey Centre Trade Pk PO4 29 G2
Pond Cotts PO8 11 E6
Pond La PO8 8 B2
Pond Piece PO7 12 B3
Ponsonby Ho PO5 5 G4
Pook La PO9 19 G6
Popham Ct PO9 14 C6
Poplar Gro PO11 32 C3
Port Royal St PO1 5 H3
Port Way PO6 23 F3
Portchester Heights PO16 22 C1
Portchester Rd PO2 26 D5
Portfield Ind Est PO3 27 F2
Portfield Rd PO3 27 F2
Portland Rd, Southsea PO5 28 D5
Portland Rd, Waterlooville PO7 17 G1
Portland St PO1 4 D2
Portland Ter PO5 28 D5
Portlands Cl GU32 7 F2
Portobello Gro PO16 22 D2
Portsdown Av PO6 25 F3
Portsdown Hill Rd, Havant PO9 18 A4
Portsdown Hill Rd, Portsmouth PO6 24 A1
Portsdown Rd PO6 22 D3
Portsdown Technology Pk PO17 23 G1
Portsmouth Rd, Portsmouth PO6 24 B5
Portsmouth Rd, Waterlooville PO8 11 C7
Portsview Av PO16 22 C2
Portsview Gdns PO16 22 C2
Portswood Rd, Havant PO9 14 D5
Portswood Rd, Portsmouth PO2 24 B6
Posbrooke Rd PO4 29 H3
Post Office Rd PO17 17 F4
Postern Cl PO16 22 C3
Potash Ter PO9 19 E4
Poulner Ct PO9 14 C5
Poulton Ct PO11 33 E5
Pound Lea PO11 32 C2
Pounds Ter PO1 4 D1
Power Rd PO1 29 F1
Powerscourt Rd PO2 26 C5
Poynings PI PO1 4 D6
Preston Rd PO2 27 E4
Pretoria Rd PO4 29 G4
Prettyjohn Ho PO4 30 A5
Primrose Ct PO7 14 A6
Prince Albert Rd PO4 29 H4
Prince George St, Havant PO9 19 F4
Prince George St, Portsmouth PO1 4 D2
Prince of Wales Cl PO7 14 A4
Princes Cl PO7 14 A3
Princes PI PO1 26 C6
Princes Rd GU32 6 B3
Princes St PO1 26 B6
Princess Gdns PO8 15 F4
Prinsted Cres PO6 25 F4
Prinsted Ct PO10 21 G5
Prinsted La PO10 36 E1
Priors Cl PO10 21 H5
Priorsdean Av PO9 29 H1
Priorsdean Cres PO9 18 D2
Priory Cres PO9 29 H3
Priory Ct PO6 22 D3
Priory Gdns, Fareham PO16 22 B3
Priory Gdns, Waterlooville PO7 13 G6
Priory Rd PO4 29 H5
Privett Ho PO1 4 D1
Privett Rd PO7 17 F6
Prochurch Rd PO8 11 C7
Proctor La PO1 29 G2
Promenade PO11 33 E6
Prospect La PO9 15 G6
Prospect Rd PO2 26 B6
Puffin Walk PO8 13 F3
Pulens Cres GU31 7 F3
Pulens La GU31 7 F2

Pump La PO8 11 C7
Purbrook Chase Precinct PO7 17 G6
Purbrook Gdns PO7 17 E4
Purbrook Heath Rd PO7 16 B4
Purbrook Rd PO1 29 F2
Purbrook Way PO7 17 H5
Purcell Cl PO7 17 H3
Pycroft Cl PO7 34 D4
Pye St PO1 5 G1
Pyle Cl PO8 11 B7
Pyramid Centre PO3 27 G2
Pyrford Cl PO7 13 G4

Quadra Point PO3 27 F1
Quail Way PO8 11 C5
Quarely Rd PO9 14 C6
Quarry Cotts PO7 9 B3
Quarterdeck Av PO4 26 A4
Quartermaine Rd PO3 27 F2
Quartermaine Rd Ind Est PO3 27 F3
Queen Annes Dr PO9 18 C3
Queen Mary Rd PO16 22 C3
Queen St, Emsworth PO10 20 D6
Queen St, Portsmouth PO1 4 C2
Queens Cres PO8 11 D5
Queens Gro, Southsea PO5 28 D5
Queens Gro, Waterlooville PO7 17 F4
Queens PI PO5 5 G6
Queens Rd, North End PO2 26 C5
Queens Rd, Petersfield GU32 6 B4
Queens Rd, Portsmouth PO1 4 C1
Queens Rd, Waterlooville PO7 13 H5
Queens Way PO5 28 D4
Queensway PO11 34 B4
Quinton Cl PO5 5 H3
Quintrell Av PO16 22 A3

Race Course La PO6 23 G3
Racton Av PO6 25 E3
Racton Rd PO10 20 D3
Radnor St PO5 5 G4
Raglan St PO5 5 H3
Rails La PO11 32 D4
Railway Flats PO1 29 F2
Railway Triangle Ind Est PO6 25 E5
Railway Vw PO1 5 H2
Raleigh Ho PO1 4 B3
Ramblers Way PO7 14 B3
Rampart Gdns PO3 24 B6
Rams Walk GU32 6 C4
Ramsdale Av PO9 14 C6
Ramsey Rd PO11 32 C4
Ramshill GU31 6 D3
Ramshill Ho GU31 6 D3
Randolph Rd PO2 26 D2
Ranelagh Rd, Havant PO9 18 D4
Ranelagh Rd, Portsmouth PO2 26 B4
Range Grn PO2 26 B2
Rapson Cl PO6 23 H2
Ravelin Ho PO1 5 E5
Raven Cft PO5 5 F6
Ravenswood Gdns PO5 29 E5
Rawlinson Ter PO1 4 D1
Ray Cl GU31 6 D3
Raymond Rd PO8 22 D2
Readon Cl GU31 6 D3
Record Rd PO10 20 B5
Rectory Av PO6 25 H2
Rectory Rd PO9 19 F5
Red Barn Av PO16 22 B2
Redbridge Gro PO9 18 D2
Redcar Av PO3 27 F4
Redcliffe Gdns PO4 29 F6
Redhill Rd PO9 15 G3
Redlands Gro PO4 30 B3
Redlands La PO10 20 D2
Redlynch Cl PO7 19 G2
Rednal Ho PO5 5 H3
Redshank Rd PO8 11 C5
Redwing Ct PO4 30 A2
Redwing Rd PO8 8 C1

Redwood Ct*,
Freshfield Gdns PO7 17 G1
Redwood Dr PO16 22 A2
Redwood Gro PO9 19 G1
Reedling Dr PO4 30 B2
Reedmace Cl PO7 14 A5
Regal Cl PO6 24 C3
Regency Ct, Portsmouth PO1 4 C5
Regency Ct, Waterlooville PO7 12 C2
Regency Gdns PO7 17 F2
Regent Mews GU32 6 A4
Regent PI PO5 5 F6
Regent St PO1 26 B6
Regents Ct PO9 19 F6
Reginald Rd PO4 29 H4
Relay Rd PO7 17 F1
Renny Rd PO1 29 F2
Renown Gdns PO8 11 A7
Reservoir La GU32 6 C2
Rest A Wyle Av PO11 32 C2
Revenge Cl PO4 30 B1
Rhinefield Cl PO9 18 B2
Richmond Cl PO11 32 A3
Richmond Dr PO11 32 A3
Richmond PI, Portsmouth PO1 4 D3
Richmond PI, Southsea PO5 28 D5
Richmond Rd PO5 29 E5
Richmond Rise PO16 22 B2
Riders La PO9 19 E1
Ridge Cl PO8 8 C4
Ridge Common La GU32 6 A1
Ridgeway Cl PO6 23 E1
Ridgeway Office Pk GU32 6 A5
Ridgway PO9 18 D5
Rimington Rd PO9 13 H4
Ringwood Ho PO9 19 F1
Ringwood Rd PO4 30 A4
Ripley Gro PO3 27 F5
Ripon Gdns PO7 14 B2
Ritchie Cl PO11 32 C4
Rival Moor Rd GU32 7 E5
River St PO10 21 E1
River Way PO9 19 F3
Riverdale Av PO7 14 A4
Riverhead Ct PO4 30 A2
Rivermead Ct PO10 20 D3
Rivers St PO5 5 H4
Riversdale Gdns PO9 19 F4
Riverside Cotts PO10 21 G1
Road Vw PO2 26 B5
Roads Hill PO8 10 B3
Robert Mack Ct PO1 4 D3
Robin Gdns PO8 13 F3
Robina Cl PO7 14 A5
Robinson Ct PO16 22 B2
Robinson Way PO3 27 G2
Rochester Rd PO4 29 G4
Rochford Rd PO6 24 A3
Rockbourne Cl PO9 18 C1
Rockingham Way PO16 22 A2
Rockrose Way PO8 23 F1
Rockville Dr PO7 17 G2
Rodney Rd PO4 29 G2
Rodney Way PO8 11 C5
Roebuck Cl PO9 24 B4
Rogate Gdns PO16 22 B1
Rogate Ho PO1 5 H1
Rogers Mead PO11 34 B4
Roland Cl PO8 11 D6
Roman Cl PO10 21 G5
Roman Grn PO7 12 A3
Roman Gro PO16 22 C5
Roman Way PO9 18 C3
Romsey Av PO3 30 A1
Romsey Rd PO8 10 E1
Rooke Ho PO1 4 D2
Rookes Cl PO8 11 D6
Rookes Mews GU31 6 D4
Rooksbury Cft PO9 15 F6
Rookwood Vw PO7 12 B2
Ropley Rd PO9 19 G1
Rose Hill PO8 11 B6
Rosebay Cl PO7 17 H3
Rosebery Av PO6 24 C4
Roselands PO8 11 B7
Rosemary La PO1 4 C3
Rosemary Way PO8 11 C7
Rosetta Rd PO4 30 A3
Rosewood Gdns PO8 8 C3
Rosina Cl PO7 13 G4
Roslyn Ho PO5 5 G5
Rostrevor La PO4 29 F6
Rother Cl GU31 7 F3

Rotherbrook Ct GU32 6 A5
Rotherwick Cl PO9 15 H6
Rothwell Cl PO9 23 F2
Roundhouse Ct PO11 32 D5
Roundhouse Mdw PO10 21 E6
Roundway PO7 13 H6
Rowan Av PO8 14 B2
Rowan Ct PO4 29 G3
Rowan Rd PO9 19 H2
Rowbury Rd PO9 14 D5
Rowes Alley PO1 4 B5
Rowin Cl PO11 33 F5
Rowland Rd PO6 22 D2
Rowlands Av PO7 13 G6
Rowlands Castle Rd PO8 11 F5
Rownhams Rd PO9 14 D6
Royal Gate PO4 30 A5
Royal Gdns PO9 9 A6
Royal Way PO7 14 A4
Ruby Ct PO7 13 G6
Rudgwick Cl PO16 22 A3
Rudmore Ct*,
Simpson Rd PO2 26 B5
Rudmore Rd PO2 26 B5
Rudmore Sq PO2 26 B4
Rugby Rd PO5 29 F3
Rushes Fm GU32 6 B3
Rushes Rd GU32 6 B3
Rushmere Walk PO9 14 D5
Rushmore Cotts PO8 11 E6
Ruskin Rd PO4 29 G3
Ruskin Way PO8 11 B8
Russell Rd PO9 19 F3
Russell Way GU32 6 D6
Russet Gdns PO10 21 E5
Rustington Ho PO1 5 G2
Rydal Cl PO6 23 G2
Ryecroft PO9 19 H4
Ryefield Cl GU31 7 F5
Ryefield Cotts GU31 7 H6

Sabre Rd PO10 36 B4
Sackville St PO5 5 F4
Sadlers Walk PO10 20 D5
Sage Cl PO7 14 A6
St Agathas Way PO1 5 F1
St Albans Rd, Havant PO9 19 G1
St Albans Rd, Southsea PO4 29 G4
St Andrew Cl PO8 10 E2
St Andrews Cl PO11 5 E3
St Andrews Rd, Hayling Island PO11 32 D5
St Andrews Rd, Portsmouth PO6 25 H3
St Anns Rd, Southsea PO5 5 H6
St Anns Rd, Southsea PO4 29 G4
St Anns Rd, Waterlooville PO8 11 D5
St Aubins Pk PO11 31 H4
St Augustine Rd PO4 29 G5
St Barbara Way PO2 27 E1
St Bartholomews Gdns PO5 29 E4
St Catherine St PO5 29 E4
St Catherines Rd PO11 31 G4
St Chads Av PO2 26 D3
St Christophers Rd PO9 18 C2
St Clares Av PO9 14 C4
St Clares Cl PO9 14 D6
St Colmans Av PO6 24 C3
St Davids Rd, Southsea PO5 5 H5
St Davids Rd, Waterlooville PO8 8 C3
St Denys Walk PO9 14 D5
St Edwards Rd PO5 5 F6
St Faiths Rd PO1 5 H1
St Francis Ct PO2 26 D1
St Francis PI PO9 19 E2
St Georges Av PO9 19 H4
St Georges Bsns Centre PO1 4 D3
St Georges Ct PO5 5 F6
St Georges Ind Est PO4 29 H2
St Georges Rd, Cosham PO6 24 C3
St Georges Rd, Hayling Island PO11 31 H4
St Georges Rd, Portsmouth PO1 4 C5

St Georges Rd, Southsea PO4 29 H5
St Georges Sq PO1 4 D3
St Georges Walk PO7 17 G1
St Georges Way PO1 4 D3
St Giles Way PO8 10 E2
St Helena Way PO16 22 B3
St Helens Cl PO4 29 F5
St Helens Par PO4 29 F6
St Helens Park Cres PO4 29 F6
St Helens Rd PO11 31 H4
St Hellens Rd PO6 25 F3
St Hermans Rd PO11 33 E5
St Hilda Av PO8 10 E2
St Hubert Rd PO8 10 E2
St James Cl PO8 8 D4
St James Rd PO10 20 C5
St James' Rd PO5 5 G4
St James St PO1 4 D2
St James Way PO16 22 B3
St Johns Av PO7 17 G5
St Johns Cl PO11 32 B5
St Johns Mews PO5 5 H6
St Johns Rd, Emsworth PO10 21 G5
St Johns Rd, Havant PO9 18 C2
St Johns Rd, Portsmouth PO6 24 C3
St Judes Cl PO5 28 D4
St Leonards Av PO11 32 C4
St Margarets Rd PO11 32 C4
St Marks Rd PO2 26 C4
St Marys Ho PO3 29 G1
St Marys Rd, Hayling Island PO11 32 B4
St Marys Rd, Portsmouth PO1 29 F1
St Matthews Rd PO6 24 C3
St Michaels Rd, Havant PO9 18 C2
St Michaels Rd, Portsmouth PO1 5 E4
St Michaels Way PO8 10 E2
St Nicholas Rd PO9 18 C2
St Nicholas St PO1 4 D6
St Pauls Rd PO5 5 F5
St Pauls Sq PO5 5 F5
St Peters Av PO11 35 D5
St Peters Ct GU32 6 C5
St Peters Gro PO5 5 H6
St Peters Rd, Hayling Island PO11 34 D3
St Peters Rd, Petersfield GU31 6 C4
St Peters Sq PO10 20 D6
St Pirans Av PO3 27 F6
St Ronans Av PO4 29 F5
St Ronans Rd PO4 29 F5
St Simons Rd PO5 29 E6
St Stephens Rd PO2 26 C5
St Swithuns Rd PO2 27 E3
St Theresas Cl PO9 18 C3
St Thomas Av PO11 31 H4
St Thomas Ct PO1 4 D5
St Thomas St PO1 4 C5
St Ursula Gro PO5 5 H6
St Vincent Cres PO8 11 C5
St Vincent Rd PO5 29 E5
St Vincent St PO5 5 F4
Salcombe Av PO3 27 F4
Salerno Rd PO2 26 C1
Salet Way PO7 14 B3
Salisbury Rd, Portsmouth PO6 24 C4
Salisbury Rd, Southsea PO4 29 G5
Salterns Av PO4 30 A2
Salterns Cl PO11 33 E4
Salterns La PO11 32 D4
Saltmarsh La PO11 32 A2
Salvia Cl PO7 14 A5
Sampson Rd PO1 4 C1
Samuel Rd PO1 29 F1
Sandalwood Cl PO8 8 C3
Sanderling Rd PO4 30 B2
Sandleford Rd PO9 14 D5
Sandown Rd PO6 24 B4
Sandpiper Cl PO8 11 C5
Sandpipers PO6 25 H3
Sandport Gro PO16 22 A4
Sandringham La PO1 29 F2
Sandringham Rd, Petersfield GU32 6 C3
Sandringham Rd, Portsmouth PO1 29 F2
Sandy Beach Est PO11 33 G6
Sandy Brow PO7 17 G6
Sandy Cl GU31 7 G5
Sandy Point Rd PO11 33 F6
Sandyfield Cres PO8 13 G4
Sapphire Ridge PO7 14 B4
Sarah Robinson Ho PO1 4 D2
Saunders Ho PO6 22 D2
Saunders Mews PO4 30 A5
Saxley Ct PO9 14 C5
Saxon Cl, Fareham PO16 22 A1
Saxon Cl, Waterlooville PO8 8 C4
Scarff Ct PO11 32 D5
Scholars Walk PO6 25 E4
School La, Emsworth PO10 20 D6
School La, Petersfield GU32 7 E2
School La, Waterlooville PO7 12 A1
School La, Westbourne PO10 21 E1
School Rd PO9 19 E5
Schooner Way PO4 30 B1
Scotney Ct PO9 15 G6
Scott Ho PO2 26 B3
Scott Rd, Hilsea PO3 24 C6
Scott Rd, Portsmouth PO1 4 B1
Scratchface La, Brockhampton PO9 18 B3
Scratchface La, Waterlooville PO7 17 H5
Sea Front PO11 31 H4
Sea Front Est PO11 32 D5
Sea Mill Gdns PO1 4 D3
Sea View Rd PO6 25 E2
Seafarers Walk PO11 33 G6
Seafield Rd, Fareham PO16 22 A4
Seafield Rd, Portsmouth PO3 27 E4
Seafields PO10 20 C6
Seagers Ct PO1 4 B5
Seagrove Av PO11 32 C5
Seagrove Rd PO2 26 C4
Seagull Cl PO4 30 B1
Seagull La PO10 20 D5
Seaton Av PO3 27 F5
Seaview Av PO16 22 D2
Seaview Cotts PO10 20 D6
Seaview Rd PO11 33 E4
Seaway Cres PO4 30 B3
Seaway Gro PO16 22 B5
Sebastian Gro PO7 14 A3
Second Av, Cosham PO6 24 B3
Second Av, Emsworth PO10 21 G5
Second Av, Farlington PO6 25 G3
Second Av, Havant PO9 19 G4
Sedgefield Cl PO6 22 D3
Sedgley Cl PO5 5 H4
Selangor Av PO10 20 A5
Selborne Av PO9 18 C1
Selborne Cl GU32 6 D2
Selbourne Rd PO9 19 E5
Selbourne Ter PO1 29 F2
Selsey Av PO4 29 H5
Selsey Cl PO11 33 H5
Selsmore Av PO11 33 E5
Selsmore Rd PO11 32 C4
Sennen Pl PO6 23 F4
Sentinel Cl PO7 14 B3
Serpentine Rd, Southsea PO5 28 D5
Serpentine Rd, Waterlooville PO7 17 E5
Serpentine Way PO5 28 D5
Service Rd PO6 23 H3
Settlers Cl PO1 5 H1
Sevenoaks Rd PO6 24 B3
Severn Cl PO6 23 G2
Seymour Cl PO2 26 C6
Shadwell Ct*, Winstanley Rd PO2 26 B3
Shadwell Rd PO2 26 C3
Shaftesbury Av PO7 17 F4
Shaftesbury Rd PO5 28 D5
Shakespeare Gdns PO8 13 G3
Shakespeare Rd PO1 29 F1
Shanklin Rd PO4 29 F3
Sharps Cl PO3 27 F1
Sharps Rd PO9 19 G1
Shawcross Ind Pk PO3 24 C6
Shawfield Rd PO9 19 G5
Shawford Gro PO9 14 C6
Shear Hill GU32 7 E3
Shearer Rd PO1 29 F1
Shearwater Dr PO6 25 H3
Sheep St GU32 6 C5
Sheepwash La PO7 12 B6
Sheepwash Rd, Cowplain PO8 11 D8
Sheepwash Rd, Horndean PO8 11 E6
Sheet Link GU32 6 D1
Sheffield Rd PO1 29 F1
Shelford Rd PO4 30 A2
Shelley Av PO6 22 D2
Shelley Gdns PO8 11 A8
Sheppard Cl PO8 11 B5
Sherfield Av PO9 15 F6
Sheringham Rd PO6 24 A2
Sherwood PO8 8 C3
Shetland Cl PO6 24 C2
Shillinglee PO7 17 G5
Ship Leopard St PO1 4 C2
Shire Cl PO7 14 B2
Shirley Av PO4 30 A3
Shirley Rd PO5 29 F5
Sholing Ct PO9 14 D5
Shore Av PO4 30 A1
Shorehaven PO6 23 E3
Short Row PO1 4 C1
Shrubbery Cl PO16 22 B4
Sidings Ter PO4 29 G3
Sidlesham Cl PO11 33 H5
Sidmouth Av PO3 27 F5
Silchester Rd PO3 27 F5
Silkstead Av PO9 15 E5
Silver St PO5 5 F6
Silverdale Cotts PO10 21 E1
Silverdale Dr PO7 13 E4
Silversands Gdns PO11 32 D5
Silverthorne Way PO7 17 F1
Silvertrees PO10 20 D3
Silvester Rd PO8 13 G4
Simmons Grn PO11 32 D4
Simpson Cl PO16 22 B2
Simpson Rd, Cosham PO6 24 B2
Simpson Rd, Stamshaw PO2 26 B4
Sinah La PO11 31 G4
Singleton Gdns PO8 8 D4
Sirius Av PO1 4 C3
Sirus Ct PO5 5 F5
Siskin Gro PO7 14 A5
Siskin Rd PO4 30 B2
Sissinghurst Rd PO16 22 A4
Sixth Av PO6 24 A3
Skew Rd PO17 22 C1
Skye Cl PO6 24 C2
Skylark Ct PO4 30 B2
Slater App PO2 26 A4
Slindon Cl PO8 8 D4
Slindon Gdns PO9 19 F5
Slindon St PO1 5 G2
Slingsby Cl PO1 5 E6
Slipper Rd PO10 21 E6
Small Cl GU31 6 D2
Smallcutts Av PO10 21 G4
Smeaton St PO2 26 B3
Smith La PO10 37 E6
Snells Cnr PO8 10 E1
Snowberry Cres PO9 19 H2
Soake Rd PO7 13 E4
Soberton Dr GU31 6 D3
Soberton Rd PO9 19 E2
Soldridge Cl PO9 15 H6
Solent Dr PO11 32 B5
Solent Heights PO4 30 C4
Solent Ho PO9 19 F2
Solent Rd, Havant PO9 18 D5
Solent Rd, Portsmouth PO6 25 E3
Solent Vw PO16 22 A2
Solihull Ho PO5 5 F4
Somborne Dr PO9 19 F1
Somers Rd PO5 5 G5
Somers Rd North PO1 29 E2
Somerset Rd PO5 29 E6
Somerville Pl PO2 26 B2
Sonnet Way PO7 14 B3
Sopley Ct PO9 15 H6
Sorrel Cl PO7 14 A6
South Av PO2 24 A6
South Bay PO10 36 C4
South Cl PO9 19 F5
South La, Emsworth PO10 21 G3
South La, Waterlooville PO8 8 B3
South Normandy PO1 4 D5
South Par PO5 29 E6
South Rd, Drayton PO6 25 F4
South Rd, Fareham PO17 23 F1
South Rd, Hayling Island PO11 32 B4
South Rd, Kingston PO1 26 D6
South Rd, Waterlooville PO8 10 D2
South Spur PO17 23 G1
South St, Emsworth PO10 20 D6
South St, Havant PO9 19 F5
South St, Southsea PO5 5 F5
South Ter PO1 4 C1
South Vw PO8 11 C8
Southampton Rd PO6 22 D3
Southampton Row PO1 4 D2
Southbourne Av, Emsworth PO10 21 E6
Southbourne Av, Portsmouth PO6 25 E3
Southbrook Cl PO9 19 F6
Southbrook Rd PO9 19 F6
Southdown Rd, Portsmouth PO6 24 C3
Southdown Rd, Waterlooville PO8 10 E1
Southdown Vw PO7 13 E4
Southfield Walk PO9 14 C5
Southlands PO6 24 C3
Southleigh Gro PO11 32 B3
Southleigh Rd, Emsworth PO10 20 C2
Southleigh Rd, Havant PO9 19 G5
Southmoor La PO9 18 D5
Southsea Esp PO4 29 F6
Southsea St PO5 5 F6
Southsea Ter PO5 5 E6
Southwick Av PO16 22 D1
Southwick Hill Rd PO6 24 A1
Southwick Rd, Portsmouth PO6 23 H1
Southwick Rd, Waterlooville PO7 12 A3
Southwood Rd, Hayling Island PO11 33 E5
Southwood Rd, Portsmouth PO2 26 D1
Sovereign Cl PO4 30 B1
Sovereign Dr PO4 30 B2
Sovereign La PO7 17 G6
Sparrow Cl PO8 11 A7
Sparrowhawk Cl PO3 27 F1
Sparsholt Cl PO9 18 B1
Spartan Cl PO10 36 B4
Specks La PO4 29 H2
Speltham Hill PO7 9 C2
Spencer Cl PO11 32 C4
Spencer Gdns PO8 11 A8
Spencer Rd, Emsworth PO10 20 B2
Spencer Rd, Southsea PO4 29 G5
Spenlow Cl PO2 26 C5
Spice Quay PO1 4 C5
Spicer Ho PO1 4 D1
Spicer St PO1 5 G1
Spindle Cl PO9 19 H3
Spindle Warren PO9 19 H3
Spinnaker Cl PO11 32 B3
Spinnaker Ct PO1 4 D3
Spinnaker Dr PO2 26 C1
Spinnaker Grange PO11 34 D3
Spinnaker Ho PO6 23 F4
Spinnaker Quay PO1 4 C5
Spinnaker Vw PO9 18 A5
Spinney Cl PO8 13 G3
Spithead Heights PO4 30 C4
Spring Gdns, Emsworth PO10 20 D6
Spring Gdns, Portsmouth PO1 5 F3
Spring St PO1 5 F2
Spring Vale PO8 11 D8
Spring Walk PO1 5 F1
Springfield Cl PO9 18 B3
Springwood Av PO7 17 H3
Spruce Av PO7 14 A5
Spur Rd, Portsmouth PO6 24 B3
Spur Rd, Waterlooville PO7 17 H1
Stacey Ct PO9 14 D4
Stafford Rd, Petersfield GU32 6 D3
Stafford Rd, Southsea PO5 5 H6
Stagshorn Rd PO8 10 D4
Stakes Hill Rd PO7 17 G2
Stakes Rd PO7 17 F4
Stallard Cl PO10 20 C5
Stamford Av PO11 32 A4
Stamford St PO1 29 F1
Stamshaw Prom PO2 24 A6
Stamshaw Rd PO2 26 C4
Stanbridge Rd PO9 19 G2
Stanford Cl PO6 23 H3
Stanford Ct PO9 19 H1
Stanhope Rd PO1 5 F2
Stanley Av PO3 27 F5
Stanley La PO5 28 D5
Stanley Rd, Emsworth PO10 20 D6
Stanley Rd, Portsmouth PO2 26 B4
Stanley St PO5 28 D5
Stansted Cl PO9 9 B6
Stansted Cres PO9 15 G5
Stansted Rd PO5 29 E3
Stanswood Rd PO9 14 D5
Stanton Rd GU32 6 B3
Staple Cl PO7 13 F6
Stapleton Rd PO3 27 E5
Starina Gdns PO7 14 B3
Station Rd, Drayton PO6 25 E5
Station Rd, Fareham PO16 22 C3
Station Rd, Hayling Island PO11 32 A3
Station Rd, Petersfield GU32 6 C4
Station Rd, Portsmouth PO3 27 E5
Station St PO1 5 F2
Staunton Av PO11 31 H4
Staunton Rd PO9 18 D4
Staunton St PO1 29 E1
Stead Cl PO11 32 D4
Steel St PO5 5 F5
Steep Cl PO16 22 B1
Steerforth Cl PO2 26 C5
Stein Rd PO10 21 G3
Stephen Cl PO8 14 B2
Stewart Borrow Ho PO8 13 G3
Stewart Pl PO1 26 D6
Stewarts Grn PO7 9 B2
Stirling Av PO7 17 H2
Stirling St PO2 26 C5
Stockbridge Cl PO9 19 H1
Stockheath La PO9 19 E3
Stockheath Rd PO9 19 E1
Stockheath Way PO9 19 F2
Stone Sq PO9 19 F2
Stone St PO5 5 F6
Stonechat Cl GU31 7 F5
Stonechat Rd PO8 11 C5
Stoneham Cl GU32 6 B3
Stoneham Pk GU32 6 B3
Stoneleigh Cl PO16 22 A3
Stony La PO1 4 B1
Storrington Rd PO8 8 D3
Stour Cl GU32 6 C6
Stowe Rd PO4 30 A3
Stratfield Gdns PO9 14 D5
Stratfield Pk PO7 17 E1
Stratford Ho PO5 5 F4
Stratford Rd PO7 14 A4
Stratton Cl PO6 23 H3
Stride Av PO3 27 F6
Strode Rd PO2 26 B3
Stroud Cl PO6 23 F2
Strouden Ct PO9 14 D5
Stroudley Av PO6 25 E4
Stroudwood Rd PO9 19 F2
Stubbington Av PO2 26 C4
Sudbury Rd PO6 24 A2
Suffolk Rd PO4 29 H4
Sullivan Cl PO6 22 D3
Sullivan Way PO7 17 G4
Sultan Rd, Emsworth PO10 20 D5
Sultan Rd, Portsmouth PO2 26 B6
Summerhill Rd PO8 11 B8

Summerlands Walk*, Bramshaw Ct PO9 15 H6
Sun Ct PO5 5 H4
Sun St PO1 4 D3
Sunderton La PO8 8 C4
Sundridge Cl PO6 24 B3
Sunningdale Rd, Fareham PO16 22 C4
Sunningdale Rd, Portsmouth PO3 27 F6
Sunny Walk PO1 4 B2
Sunnyfields PO6 19 E2
Sunnyheath PO9 19 E2
Sunnymead Dr PO7 13 E5
Sunnyside Walk PO9 14 D5
Sunshine Av PO11 32 D5
Suntrap Gdns PO11 32 D5
Sunwood Rd PO9 14 D6
Surrey St PO1 5 G2
Sussex Gdns GU31 6 D5
Sussex Pl PO5 5 F6
Sussex Rd, Petersfield GU31 6 D5
Sussex Rd, Southsea PO5 5 F6
Sussex Ter PO5 28 D4
Sutherland Rd PO4 29 F4
Sutton Cl, Portsmouth PO8 27 G1
Sutton Cl, Waterlooville PO8 13 F3
Sutton Rd PO8 13 F4
Swallow Cl PO9 19 H3
Swallow Ct PO8 8 B2
Swan Cl PO10 20 D6
Swan St GU32 6 B4
Swanmore Rd PO9 14 D4
Swans Walk PO11 32 D4
Swarraton Rd PO9 19 F2
Sway Ct PO9 19 H1
Swaythling Rd PO9 14 D5
Sweetbriar Gdns PO7 17 H3
Swift Cl PO8 11 C5
Swift Rd PO10 36 C4
Swinburn Gdns PO8 11 A8
Swiss Rd PO7 17 G2
Sword Cl PO8 8 B3
Swordsands Path PO3 27 H6
Swordsands Rd PO3 27 H6
Sycamore Cl, Clanfield PO8 8 D3
Sycamore Cl, Wecock PO8 13 G4
Sycamore Dr PO11 32 B3
Sydenham Ter PO1 29 E2
Sydmonton Ct PO9 15 H6
Sydney Ho PO1 5 H1
Sylvan Vw PO7 14 A6
Sywell Cres PO3 27 G1

Tagdell La PO8 10 B4
Talbot Cl PO9 18 C3
Talbot Rd, Havant PO9 18 D3
Talbot Rd, Southsea PO4 29 F4
Tamar Down PO7 14 A4
Tamarisk Cl, Southsea PO4 30 A4
Tamarisk Cl, Waterlooville PO7 14 A6
Tamworth Rd PO3 29 H1
Tangier Rd PO3 27 F6
Tanglewood Cl PO7 17 F5
Tangley Walk*, Sharps Rd PO9 15 H6
Tankerton Cl PO6 24 A3
Tanners La PO7 12 C2
Tanners Ridge PO7 17 G6
Tansy Cl PO7 14 A5
Tarbery Cres PO8 10 E4
Target Rd PO2 23 G2
Tarleton Rd PO6 10 D1
Tarn Rise PO8 13 E3
Tarrant Gdns PO9 18 D3
Taswell Rd PO5 29 E5
Tattershall Cres PO16 22 A4
Tavistock Gdns PO9 19 H5
Teal Cl, Hayling Island PO11 32 D4
Teal Cl, Waterlooville PO8 11 C5
Teapot Row PO4 29 H5
Teazle Cl GU31 7 F5
Ted Kelly Ct PO1 4 D3
Teddington Rd PO4 29 H3
Tegdown GU32 7 E4
Teglease Grn PO9 14 D4

Teignmouth Rd PO3 27 F5
Telephone Rd PO4 29 F3
Telford Rd PO2 26 D2
Tempest Av PO7 14 A4
Temple St PO1 5 G1
Templeton Cl PO2 26 D2
Tennyson Cres PO7 13 G5
Tennyson Rd PO2 27 E5
Terence Gdns PO4 29 F5
Tern Walk PO4 30 A2
Test Cl GU32 6 B6
Testwood Rd PO9 18 D1
Tewkesbury Cl PO6 23 H3
The Admiral Pk PO3 27 F1
The Avenue GU31 6 D5
The Beeches PO7 17 H1
The Boardwalk PO6 23 G4
The Boltons PO7 17 G6
The Borough GU32 6 C5
The Brambles PO7 13 F6
The Brambles Ent Pk PO7 13 E6
The Bri Shopping Centre PO7 29 E2
The Brow PO7 25 E1
The Byre PO8 10 B1
The Causeway GU32 6 C6
The Chace Gdns PO7 17 G4
The Challenge Ent Centre PO3 27 F2
The Circle PO5 29 E5
The Circus PO17 23 F1
The Close, Fareham PO16 22 B3
The Close, Portsmouth PO6 24 D3
The Coppice PO8 11 C6
The Courtyard*, Heath Rd GU31 6 D4
The Crescent, Emsworth PO10 21 G6
The Crescent, Waterlooville PO7 17 F5
The Crest PO7 25 E1
The Crossway PO16 22 A3
The Curve PO8 11 A5
The Dale PO7 25 E1
The Dell PO9 18 B4
The Downsway PO16 22 B3
The Drift PO9 9 B6
The Drive, Emsworth PO10 21 G6
The Drive, Havant PO9 19 F3
The Droke PO6 24 C3
The Fairway, Fareham PO16 22 B3
The Fairway, Rowlands Castle PO9 9 B5
The Fishermans PO10 20 D6
The Florins PO7 17 G5
The Forum PO9 19 E4
The Gardens, Havant PO9 19 H5
The Gardens, Waterlooville PO7 9 B2
The George Ct PO1 4 D6
The Glade, Hayling Island PO11 33 E5
The Glade, Waterlooville PO7 14 A3
The Gorseway PO11 31 H4
The Green PO9 9 C5
The Greenway PO10 20 C2
The Grove PO10 21 E2
The Guelders PO7 17 G6
The Hard PO1 4 C2
The Hard Interchange PO1 4 C3
The Hassocks PO7 14 A4
The Haven PO4 30 A2
The Heath PO7 12 C2
The Hillway PO16 13 F5
The Hundred PO7 13 F5
The Keep PO16 22 C3
The Kingsway PO16 22 B3
The Lane PO4 29 G5
The Leaway PO7 22 C3
The Liberty PO7 12 B3
The Lighthouse PO11 4 C4
The Limes PO4 19 F6
The Link PO7 14 A3
The Lodge PO7 14 A6
The Mall PO2 5 F6
The Mallards PO9 19 E6
The Maltings GU31 6 D5
The Mary Rose St PO1 5 G3
The Mead GU32 6 B5

The Meadow PO7 12 B3
The Meadows PO7 13 E6
The Mews, Langstone PO9 34 A1
The Mews, Petersfield GU31 6 D3
The Mews, Stockheath PO9 19 E2
The Nelson Centre PO3 27 F2
The Oaks PO8 14 A1
The Oakwood Centre PO9 19 H2
The Old Flour Mill PO10 20 D6
The Old Rd PO6 24 B5
The Orchard, Portsmouth PO6 24 C4
The Orchard, Waterlooville PO7 12 B3
The Oyster Est PO6 25 F4
The Pallant PO9 19 F4
The Parade PO1 4 C1
The Paradechment PO9 19 F5
The Pastures PO7 12 B3
The Peak PO9 9 B5
The Precinct PO7 17 G1
The Promenade PO10 36 B1
The Purrocks GU32 6 C2
The Queensway PO16 22 A3
The Retreat PO5 5 G6
The Ridings PO2 27 E1
The Rise PO7 17 F6
The Rookery PO10 20 D5
The Saltings, Langstone PO9 34 B1
The Saltings, Portsmouth PO6 25 H4
The Sanderlings PO11 32 C5
The Slipway PO6 23 F4
The Smithy PO7 12 B3
The Spain GU32 6 C4
The Spinney, Denmead PO7 12 B4
The Spinney, Horndean PO8 11 C6
The Spring PO7 12 C3
The Square, Petersfield GU32 6 C4
The Square, Southbourne PO10 21 G6
The Square, Westbourne PO10 21 E2
The Strand PO11 33 E6
The Tanneries Ind Est PO9 19 E5
The Thicket, Southsea PO5 5 G6
The Thicket, Waterlooville PO7 17 F6
The Tithe PO7 12 B3
The Vale, Southsea PO4 28 D5
The Vale, Waterlooville PO7 10 D2
The Vulcan PO1 4 C4
The Warrior Bsns Centre PO6 25 G4
The Westbrook PO7 14 B2
The Willows PO7 12 B3
The Wren Centre PO10 21 E2
The Yews PO8 10 E4
Thieves La PO8 8 D1
Third Av, Havant PO9 19 G4
Third Av, Portsmouth PO6 24 B3
Thistle Down PO8 11 C7
Thistledowne Gdns PO10 21 E5
Thomas Parr Ho PO6 24 A3
Thomas Rd GU31 6 D3
Thorn Cl GU31 7 F5
Thorncliffe Cl PO2 27 E1
Thorncroft Rd PO1 29 F2
Thorney Rd PO10 21 E6
Thornfield Cl PO8 10 E1
Thornham La PO10 36 D1
Thornton Cl PO7 25 E1
Thornton Rd PO7 12 C3
Three Acres PO8 10 E4
Three Tun Cl PO1 4 D3
Thresher Cl PO7 14 B3
Thrush Walk PO8 11 A8
Thruxton Rd PO9 14 C6
Thurbern Rd PO2 26 D3

Tichborne Gro PO9 14 C6
Tidcombe Grn PO9 14 C5
Tideway Gdns PO4 30 B3
Tidworth Rd PO9 19 E1
Tiffield Cl PO3 27 G1
Tilford Rd PO8 11 B6
Tillington Gdns PO8 8 D4
Tilmore Gdns GU32 6 C2
Tilmore Rd GU32 6 C3
Timberlane PO7 17 G5
Timpson Rd PO1 29 E1
Timsbury Cres PO9 18 D3
Tintagel Way PO6 23 G4
Tinton Cl PO6 23 E1
Tipner Grn PO2 26 B2
Tipner La PO2 26 A2
Tipner Rd PO2 26 B3
Tiptoe Grn*, Burghclere Rd PO9 15 H6
Tipton Ho PO5 5 G4
Tisted Ct PO9 15 H6
Titus Gdns PO7 14 A4
Toby St PO1 5 G1
Tobys Gdn GU31 6 D5
Todhurst Ho PO7 15 H3
Togo Av PO1 4 C3
Tokar St PO4 29 H5
Tokio Rd PO3 27 E4
Tonbridge St PO5 28 D5
Topaz Gro PO7 14 B3
Tor Way GU31 6 D4
Torberry Dr GU32 7 E5
Torfrida Ct PO4 30 B4
Toronto Rd PO2 26 D6
Torrington Rd PO2 26 D2
Totland Rd PO6 24 B3
Tottenham Rd PO1 29 F1
Totton Walk PO9 14 D5
Tournerbury La PO11 32 C3
Tower Gdns PO9 34 B1
Tower Rd PO4 29 G4
Tower St, Emsworth PO10 20 D6
Tower St, Portsmouth PO1 4 B5
Town Hall Rd PO9 19 F5
Town La PO32 7 E2
Towpath Mead PO4 30 B3
Trafalgar Cl PO10 21 G6
Trafalgar Pl PO1 29 F1
Trafalgar Rise PO8 8 B3
Tranmere Rd PO4 30 A3
Tredegar Rd PO4 29 G4
Treeside Way PO7 13 G5
Trefoil Cl PO7 14 A5
Tregaron Av PO6 24 D3
Treloar Rd PO11 33 G6
Trevis Rd PO4 30 A3
Trevor Rd PO4 29 F4
Trimmers Ct PO1 17 H6
Trojan Way PO7 17 H6
Troon Cres PO6 25 E2
Trosnant Rd PO9 19 E3
Truro Rd PO6 20 C2
Tudor Av PO10 20 C2
Tudor Cl, Fareham PO16 22 A1
Tudor Cl, Hayling Island PO11 32 B5
Tudor Cres PO6 24 B5
Tulip Gdns PO9 18 C4
Tunstall Rd PO6 24 A2
Tunworth Ct PO9 19 H1
Tuppenny La PO10 21 F6
Turner Rd PO1 26 C6
Tuscany Way PO7 14 B3
Tweed Ct PO9 19 E1
Twyford Av PO2 26 C4
Tyler Ct PO9 19 E1
Tyrrel Lawn PO9 14 D4
Tyseley Rd PO5 5 G3
Tytherley Grn*, Prospect La PO9 15 G6

Underdown Av PO7 25 F1
Unicorn Rd PO1 5 F1
Union Pl PO1 29 E1
Union Rd PO9 19 E4
Union St PO1 4 C3
Uplands Rd, Portsmouth PO6 25 E2
Uplands Rd, Rowlands Castle PO9 9 C5
Upper Arundel St PO1 5 G2
Upper Bere Wood PO7 17 H2
Upper Chapters PO7 9 B2
Upper Cornaway La PO16 22 A2
Upper Heyshott GU31 6 D4

Upper Piece PO7 12 D3
Upper Wardown GU32 7 E3
Upton Cl PO10 14 D5
Valentine Ct PO7 14 A4
Valetta Pk PO10 20 C5
Valetta Rd PO10 37 E6
Valiant Gdns PO2 26 C1
Valiant Rd PO10 37 E6
Valley Cl PO7 17 E6
Valley Park Dr PO8 8 D4
Vanguard Ct PO4 30 B4
Varsity Rd PO10 37 F6
Vauxhall Way GU32 6 B4
Vectis Way PO6 24 B4
Velder Av PO4 29 H2
Venice Cl PO7 14 A3
Ventnor Rd PO4 29 F3
Venture Ct PO3 24 D6
Venture Ind Pk PO3 24 D6
Verbena Cres PO8 11 D7
Vernon Av, Portsmouth PO1 4 C4
Vernon Av, Southsea PO4 29 H2
Vernon Ct PO2 26 D3
Vernon Mews PO4 29 H2
Vernon Rd PO3 27 E3
Verwood Rd PO9 15 G6
Vian Rd PO7 17 G3
Vicarage La PO7 9 C2
Viceroy Ct GU32 6 B5
Victor Rd, Emsworth PO10 37 E6
Victor Rd, Portsmouth PO3 27 E6
Victoria Av, Hayling Island PO11 32 B4
Victoria Av, Portsmouth PO1 28 C4
Victoria Av, Southsea PO5 5 F6
Victoria Av, Waterlooville PO7 17 E6
Victoria Gro PO5 5 H6
Victoria Rd, Emsworth PO10 20 B5
Victoria Rd, Hayling Island PO11 35 B5
Victoria Rd, Portsmouth PO1 28 B1
Victoria Rd, Waterlooville PO7 17 G2
Victoria Rd North PO5 5 H6
Victoria Rd South PO5 29 E5
Victoria Ter PO10 21 G6
Victoria Ter*, East St PO10 21 E2
Victory Av PO8 11 B6
Victory Grn PO2 26 B2
Victory Ho PO6 23 F4
Victory Rd PO1 4 C3
Victory Retail Pk PO1 26 B6
Victory Trading Est PO3 27 F3
Viking Way PO8 10 E1
Villa Gdns PO7 17 H1
Village St GU32 7 E2
Villiers Rd PO5 28 D5
Vincent Gro PO16 22 B4
Vine Coppice PO7 17 G4
Vita Rd PO2 26 D2
Vivash Rd PO1 29 F2
Vulcan Rd PO10 37 F6

Wade Court Rd PO9 19 G6
Wade La PO9 34 B1
Wadham Rd PO2 26 C3
Wagtail Rd PO8 11 C5
Wainscott Rd PO4 29 H5
Wainwright Cl PO6 25 F1
Wait End Rd PO7 17 G3
Wakefield Ct PO7 17 H6
Wakefords Way PO9 15 G5
Walberton Av PO6 24 C3
Walburton Way PO8 11 C8
Walden Gdns PO8 8 C4
Walden Rd PO2 26 D3
Walford Rd PO6 23 H2
Walker Rd PO2 27 E4
Wallace Rd PO2 27 E4
Wallington Rd PO2 27 E4
Wallis Gdns PO7 13 H6
Wallis Rd PO7 13 G6
Wallisdean Av PO3 27 E5

Wallrock Walk PO10 20 C2
Walmer Rd PO1 29 F2
Walnut Tree Cl PO11 32 B4
Walnut Tree Dr PO10 21 H2
Walsall Rd PO3 29 H1
Walsingham Cl PO10 24 A2
Waltham Cl PO16 22 B1
Waltham St PO5 5 F4
Walton Cl PO17 17 G3
Walton Ct PO1 4 C5
Walton Mews PO1 17 G3
Walton Rd PO6 25 E5
Walton Rd Ind Est PO6 25 E5
Warbler Cl PO8 11 C5
Warblington Av PO9 19 H5
Warblington Ct PO1 4 B5
Warblington Rd PO10 20 B6
Warblington St PO1 4 D5
Warbrook Ct PO9 15 H6
Ward Cres PO10 20 D3
Ward Cl, Emsworth PO10 21 E5
Ward Cl, Hayling Island PO11 32 A5
Ward Ho PO1 4 D1
Wardens Cl PO11 32 B2
Wardroom Rd PO2 26 A4
Warfield Av PO7 17 G2
Warfield Cres PO7 17 H2
Warnborough Ct PO9 15 H6
Warnford Cres PO9 14 D6
Warren Av PO4 29 H2
Warren Cl PO11 31 G3
Warsash Cl PO9 15 E5
Warspite Cl PO2 26 C1
Warwick Cres PO5 5 G4
Warwick Ct*, Kings Ter PO10 20 D5
Wasdale Cl PO8 10 D2
Washbrook Rd PO6 24 A2
Washington Rd, Emsworth PO10 20 C5
Washington Rd, Portsmouth PO2 26 C5
Waterberry Dr PO7 13 E6
Waterlock Gdns PO10 30 B3
Waterloo Cl PO8 13 F3
Waterloo Rd PO9 19 F4
Waterloo St PO5 5 G4
Watermead Rd PO6 25 H3
Watermill Ct*, Bulbeck Rd PO9 19 F5
Waters Edge Gdns PO10 20 C6
Watersedge Rd PO6 23 F3
Waterside La PO16 22 D5
Waterworks Rd, Petersfield GU32 6 D1
Waterworks Rd, Portsmouth PO6 25 G3
Watts Rd PO1 26 C6
Waverley Gro PO4 29 F5
Waverley Rd, Portsmouth PO6 25 E3
Waverley Rd, Southsea PO5 29 E6
Wayfarer Cl PO4 30 B2
Wayfarers Walk PO7 12 B1
Wayte St PO6 24 B3
Weavers Grn PO9 20 A3
Webb Cl PO11 32 C5
Webb La PO11 32 C5
Webb Rd PO16 22 C5
Wedgewood Way PO8 13 G4
Welch Rd PO4 29 F5
Welchwood Cl PO8 11 B6
Well Copse Cl PO8 10 E2
Well Mdw PO9 15 E5
Wellesley Cl PO7 17 G2
Wellington Cl PO8 11 F6
Wellington Gr PO16 22 B3
Wellington Retail Pk PO7 17 G1
Wellington St PO5 5 G4
Wellington Ter PO2 26 C5
Wellington Way PO7 17 G1
Wellow Cl PO9 18 D3
Wells Cl PO3 30 A1
Wellswood Gdns PO9 9 C4

Wellsworth La PO9 9 C4
Wembley Gro PO6 24 D5
Wendover Rd PO9 19 E4
Wensley Gdns PO10 20 D3
Wentworth Dr, Emsworth PO10 21 G4
Wentworth Dr, Waterlooville PO8 10 D4
Wesermarsch Rd PO8 11 B8
Wesley Gro PO3 27 E2
Wessex Gate Ind Est PO8 11 E5
Wessex Gdns PO16 22 B3
Wessex Rd PO8 10 E1
West Battery Rd PO2 26 A4
West Ct PO4 29 H4
West Haye Rd PO11 33 F6
West La, Newtown PO11 32 A3
West La, Stoke PO11 35 A8
West St, Emsworth PO10 20 D5
West St, Fareham PO16 22 A3
West St, Havant PO9 18 D4
West St, Kingston PO1 26 D6
West St, Portsmouth PO1 4 B5
West St, Waterlooville PO9 9 B2
Westbourne Av PO10 20 D4
Westbourne Cl PO10 20 D4
Westbourne Ct*, Chidham Cl PO9 19 E3
Westbourne Rd, Emsworth PO10 20 D2
Westbourne Rd, Portsmouth PO2 27 E4
Westbrook Gro PO7 17 F4
Westbrook Rd PO16 22 C5
Westbrooke Cl PO8 11 C6
Westbury Cl PO6 23 G2
Westerham Cl PO6 24 B3
Western Av PO10 20 B5
Western Par, Emsworth PO10 20 B6
Western Par, Southsea PO5 28 C4
Western Rd, Havant PO9 19 E4
Western Rd, Portsmouth PO6 23 H3
Western Ter PO3 26 B3
Westfield Ind Est PO8 11 E5
Westfield Oaks PO11 32 B4
Westfield Rd PO4 29 H4
Westgrove Gdns PO10 20 C5
Westland Dr PO7 17 H4
Westlands Gro PO16 22 B4
Westmead Cl PO11 32 A4
Westminster Pl PO1 26 C6
Weston Av PO9 29 H3
Weston Cl PO1 5 H2
Weston Ho GU32 6 B5
Weston Rd GU31 6 D5
Westover Rd PO3 27 F5
Westside Vw PO7 13 F6
Westways PO9 25 H3
Westwood Cl PO10 20 D3
Westwood Rd PO2 26 D1
Wetherdown GU32 7 E4
Weyhill Cl, Fareham PO16 22 B1
Weyhill Cl, Havant PO9 14 D6
Weymouth Rd PO2 26 C3
Whaddon Ct PO9 14 C6
Whale Island Way PO2 26 B4
Whaley Rd PO2 26 A4
Wharf Rd PO2 26 B5
Wheatear Dr GU31 7 G5
Wheatlands Av PO11 33 F6
Wheatlands Cres PO11 33 G6
Wheatley Grn PO10 14 C6
Wheatsheaf Dr PO8 13 F3

Wheatstone Rd PO4 29 F4
Wherwell Ct PO9 15 H6
Whichers Cl PO9 15 H4
Whichers Gate Rd PO9 15 H3
Whimbrel Cl PO4 30 B2
Whippingham Cl PO6 24 A3
Whitcombe Gdns PO3 29 G1
White Beam Rise PO8 8 C3
White Cloud Pk PO4 29 G4
White Cloud Pl PO4 29 G4
White Cross Gdns PO2 26 D1
White Dirt La PO8 10 C2
White Hart Alley PO1 4 C6
White Hart La PO16 22 A4
White Hart Rd PO1 4 C6
White Ho Gdns GU32 6 B2
White Horse La PO7 12 D1
White Ladies Cl PO9 19 G5
White Swan Rd PO1 5 E3
Whitebeam Cl PO8 11 D6
Whitechimney Row PO10 21 E3
Whitecliffe Av PO3 27 F6
Whitehaven, Fareham PO16 22 B4
Whitehaven, Waterlooville PO8 11 F6
Whitethorn Rd PO11 32 D4
Whitley Cl PO10 21 E1
Whitley Row PO4 30 B2
Whitsbury Rd PO9 15 G6
Whitstable Rd PO6 24 A3
Whittington Ct PO10 20 C5
Whitwell Rd PO4 29 F6
Whitworth Rd PO2 27 E5
Wickham St PO1 4 C2
Wickor Cl PO10 20 D3
Wickor Way PO10 20 D3
Wicor Mill La PO16 22 A4
Wicor Path PO16 22 D5
Widley Court Dr PO6 24 C4
Widley Ct PO6 24 C4
Widley Gdns PO7 17 F6
Widley Rd, Cosham PO6 24 C3
Widley Rd, Stamshaw PO2 26 B3
Widley Walk PO7 16 C5
Wield Cl PO9 18 C1
Wigan Cres PO9 18 B3
Wilberforce Rd PO5 5 F6
Wilby La PO3 27 H1
Wildmoor Walk PO9 15 H6
Wilkins Cl PO8 8 B2
Wilkinson Ho*, Gunners Pk PO4 30 A5
Willersley Cl PO6 23 H2
William Booth Ho PO1 4 D2
Williams Rd PO3 27 F2
Willis Rd PO1 5 F2
Willow Cl PO9 19 G5
Willow Gdns PO10 21 E1
Willow Tree Av PO8 14 B1
Willow Wood Rd PO11 32 C4
Willowdene Cl PO9 18 B2
Wilmcote Gdns PO5 5 H5
Wilson Gro PO5 29 E4
Wilton Dr PO8 11 C6
Wilton Pl PO5 28 D5
Wilton Ter PO5 29 E5
Wiltshire St PO5 5 E4
Wilverley Av PO9 19 G2
Wimbledon Park Rd PO5 29 E5
Wimborne Rd PO4 29 H3
Wimpole St PO1 29 E1
Wincanton Way PO7 14 B2
Winchcombe Rd PO6 23 G2
Winchester Ho PO9 19 F1
Winchester Rd, Petersfield GU32 6 A3
Winchester Rd, Portsmouth PO2 26 D5
Winchfield Cres PO9 18 B2
Windermere Rd PO2 27 E2
Windmill Cl PO8 8 C3
Windmill Field PO7 12 D2
Windmill Gro PO16 22 A4

Windrush Gdns PO9 17 F2
Windsor Ho PO1 5 H2
Windsor La PO5 5 H5
Windsor Rd, Fareham PO16 22 C4
Windsor Rd, Petersfield GU32 6 C4
Windsor Rd, Portsmouth PO6 24 C4
Windsor Rd, Waterlooville PO7 13 F5
Winfield Way PO10 20 D2
Wingfield St PO1 26 C6
Winifred Rd PO7 13 G6
Winkfield Row PO8 11 C7
Winkton Cl PO9 18 D3
Winscombe Av PO8 14 A1
Winslade Rd PO9 14 D6
Winsor Cl PO11 33 F6
Winstanley Rd PO2 26 B3
Winston Churchill Av PO1,5 5 F4
Winston Cl PO11 32 A4
Winter Rd PO4 29 G4
Winterbourne Rd PO6 23 E1
Winterhill Rd PO6 24 A3
Winterslow Dr PO9 15 E5
Winton Rd, Petersfield GU32 6 C4
Winton Rd, Portsmouth PO2 27 E3
Wisborough Rd PO5 29 E5
Wish Pl PO5 29 F4
Wisteria Gdns PO9 19 H2
Witchampton Rd PO9 19 G1
Withington Cl PO6 23 F2
Witley Rd PO8 11 A5
Wittering Rd PO11 33 H5
Wode Cl PO8 10 E1
Wolverton Rd PO9 19 E1
Wonston Ct PO9 15 H6
Woodberry La PO9 9 C5
Woodbury Av, Havant PO9 19 F6
Woodbury Av, Petersfield GU32 6 B3
Woodbury Gro PO8 11 B7
Woodcot Cres PO9 15 G6
Woodcroft Gdns PO8 11 A7
Woodcroft La PO8 11 A7
Woodfield Av PO6 25 G2
Woodfield Park Rd PO10 21 E5
Woodgaston La PO11 35 D6
Woodgreen Av PO9 18 D3
Woodhay Walk*, Burghclere Rd PO9 15 H6
Woodington Cl PO9 15 G6
Woodland St PO1 29 F1
Woodland Vw PO8 11 A6
Woodlands Av PO10 20 C3
Woodlands Cotts PO7 12 A3
Woodlands Gro PO7 17 F4
Woodlands La PO11 32 A2
Woodlands Way PO9 19 F2
Woodlark Gdns GU31 7 G5
Woodleigh Cl PO9 20 A2
Woodmancote La PO10 21 H1
Woodmancote Rd PO4 29 H3
Woodpath PO5 5 G6
Woodpath Ho PO5 5 G6
Woodpecker Cl PO9 19 H4
Woodpecker Way PO3 27 E1
Woodroffe Walk PO10 20 C2
Woodrow PO7 12 B2
Woodsedge PO7 14 A6
Woodstock Av PO8 11 B6
Woodstock Rd PO9 18 C3
Woodville Dr PO1 5 E6
Woodville Rd PO9 18 B4
Woofferton Rd PO6 23 F1
Woolmer Cl PO9 15 H6
Woolmer St PO10 20 B2
Woolner Av, Petersfield GU32 6 C3
Woolner Av, Portsmouth PO6 24 D3

Woolston Rd PO9 14 C
Wootton St PO6 24 B
Worcester Cl PO5 5 G
Wordsworth Av PO6 22 D
Worldham Rd PO9 15 H
Worsley Rd PO5 5 G
Worsley St PO4 29 H
Worthing Rd PO5 5 G
Worthy Ct PO9 19 G1
Wraysbury Park Dr PO10 20 C
Wrexham Gro PO8 10 D
Wyborn Cl PO11 32 C5
Wyeford Cl PO9 15 H6
Wykeham Av PO2 26 D
Wykeham Rd PO2 26 D
Wyllie Rd PO2 26 D1
Wymering La PO6 24 A
Wymering Manor Cl PO6 24 A3
Wymering Rd PO2 26 D5
Wyndcliffe Rd PO4 29 F4
Wyndham Cl PO8 10 D
Wyndham Mews PO1 4 D6

Yaldhurst Ct PO9 15 G6
Yapton St PO1 5 G2
Yarborough Rd PO5 5 G6
Yardlea Cl PO9 9 B6
Yardley Cl PO3 27 G1
Yateley Cl PO9 14 C6
Yeo Ct PO4 30 B4
Yew Tree Av PO8 14 B2
Yew Tree Gdns PO7 12 B2
Yew Tree Rd PO11 35 B7
Yoells Cres PO8 11 B6
Yoells La PO8 11 A6
York Cl GU32 6 B4
York Gdns PO16 22 D4
York Pl PO1 4 D2
York St PO1 5 G2
York Ter PO2 24 B6
Yorke St PO5 5 F5
Yves Mews PO5 29 E5

Zetland Rd PO6 25 F4
Zeus La PO7 17 H5